Praise for the previous editions

▌▌ Mike and Chris understand with unusual clarity what drives a start-up.
SIR TIM SMIT, FOUNDER, THE EDEN PROJECT

▌▌ Refreshing and very readable.
RICHARD DONKIN, FT

▌▌ This book, for me, says it all. It should become standard reading for all employees, managers and founders of start-up businesses.
PROFESSOR SIR CHRISTOPHER EVANS, OBE, FOUNDER, CHIROSCIENCE AND MERLIN BIOSCIENCES

▌▌ If I were to advise an aspiring company founder in any part of the world to read just one book, this would be it.
ROBERT I. SUTTON, PROFESSOR OF MANAGEMENT SCIENCE AT STANFORD ENGINEERING SCHOOL AND AUTHOR OF WEIRD IDEAS THAT WORK

▌▌ I recommend this book to any aspiring entrepreneur.
SIR CHARLES DUNSTONE CVO, FOUNDER, CARPHONE WAREHOUSE

▌▌ There was a lot of excellent advice and many useful tools which I'll be trying. I will also recommend it to our University commercialization specialists, for them to give to academics interested in spinning out an idea.

PROFESSOR L ANNE GLOVER, DEPARTMENT OF MOLECULAR AND CELL BIOLOGY, UNIVERSITY OF ABERDEEN.

" Provocative, down-to-earth and witty, too.

NAYYER HUSSAIN, CO-FOUNDER, MCGEOCH TECHNOLOGY

" There are too many half-finished books by my bed that would have helped get me there years ago if I had just finished them. Yet I read *Beermat* in just one sitting; I enjoyed the book and related to it.

SIMON WOODROFFE, FOUNDER, YO SUSHI.

" An embarrassingly accurate picture of entrepreneurs. I went round the office reading out sections, and people laughed out loud.

PETER HALL, FOUNDER, THE WADENHOE CONSULTANCY

" Jam-packed with solid advice you seldom see in other books.

TRAINING JOURNAL

" I really like this one . . . good practical stuff.

SIR GERRY ROBINSON, FORMER CHAIR / CEO GRANADA GROUP, ON BBC RADIO 4

The Beermat Entrepreneur

Pearson

At Pearson, we have a simple mission: to help people make more of their lives through learning.

We combine innovative learning technology with trusted content and educational expertise to provide engaging and effective learning experiences that serve people wherever and whenever they are learning.

From classroom to boardroom, our curriculum materials, digital learning tools and testing programmes help to educate millions of people worldwide – more than any other private enterprise.

Every day our work helps learning flourish, and wherever learning flourishes, so do people.

To learn more, please visit us at **www.pearson.com/uk**

The Beermat Entrepreneur

Turn your good idea into
a great business

Third edition

Mike Southon and Chris West

Pearson

Harlow, England • London • New York • Boston • San Francisco • Toronto • Sydney
Dubai • Singapore • Hong Kong • Tokyo • Seoul • Taipei • New Delhi
Cape Town • São Paulo • Mexico City • Madrid • Amsterdam • Munich • Paris • Milan

PEARSON EDUCATION LIMITED
KAO Two
KAO Park
Harlow
CM17 9NA
United Kingdom
Tel: +44 (0)1279 623623
Web: www.pearson.com/uk

First edition published 2002 (print)
Second edition published 2005 (print)
Third edition published 2018 (print and electronic)

ISBN: 978-1-292-24383-2 (print)
        978-1-292-24384-9 (PDF)
        978-1-292-24385-6 (ePub)

British Library Cataloguing-in-Publication Data
A catalogue record for the print edition is available from the British Library

Library of Congress Cataloging-in-Publication Data
A catalog record for the print edition is available from the Library of Congress

10 9 8 7 6 5 4 3 2 1

22 21 20 19 18

Cover design by Kit Foster

Print edition typeset in 10.25/14 pt Frutiger by SPi Global
Printed by Ashford Colour Press Ltd, Gosport

NOTE THAT ANY PAGE CROSS REFERENCES REFER TO THE PRINT EDITION

To James and Imogen and the next generation of Beermat entrepreneurs

Contents

About the authors

Mike Southon

Mike co-founded The Instruction Set, a training and software business which grew from 3 to 150 people in five years and was then acquired by Cap Gemini Ernst and Young. He then worked on two start-ups which eventually both went public, and a number which didn't. Since the first publication of *The Beermat Entrepreneur* in 2002 he has spoken at over a thousand events all over the world and provided free, face-to-face mentoring to over 1,500 aspiring entrepreneurs.

When he's not being *The Beermat Entrepreneur* at live events, Mike helps any type of company refine their elevator pitches, test their sales models and grow their sales.

"Mike is more than Quite Interesting. He spreads insight and cheerfulness in equal measure, like an ambidextrous chef icing two cakes at once." – John Lloyd, producer of *QI, Not the Nine o'Clock News, Spitting Image* and *The Hitchhiker's Guide to the Galaxy.*

Chris West

Chris is a professional writer. His first book, *Journey to the Middle Kingdom,* was published in 1991, and he has had over 20 books published since, in various genres. *The Dragon Awakens* is a quartet of crime novels set in 1990s China. *Eurovision!* tells the story of modern Europe through the lens of the Eurovision Song Contest. *Perfect Written English* is a guide to good, clear writing. He is co-author of the *Beermat Guides* to sales, finance and marketing for small businesses. He has also worked in the City, in marketing and PR for the Norwich-based MK Group, and has advised start-up enterprises.

Chris works with subject-matter experts to turn their knowledge into lively, accessible books. He is a member of United Ghostwriters, a group of top professionals in this field.

Foreword
by Priya Lakhani OBE

Winner of the Global AI Award in Education

Founder and CEO of CENTURY Tech

It's a huge pleasure to be asked to introduce the new edition of *The Beermat Entrepreneur.* It's a book I love for its directness and candour. It's like a friend giving you advice. Yes, that advice can be opinionated, but I don't want someone telling me there are hundreds of things I could do. I want expert, hard-earned, personal opinion – after which, of course, like all entrepreneurs, I will make my own mind up.

Mike has been down this road, and can advise not just about starting up, but about the choices to be made as the business grows, and even when or if you should sell.

Beermat stresses perhaps the deepest truth about business, that it is about people. I run a company that is driven by technological innovation. CENTURY Tech uses the latest AI techniques to revolutionise and personalise education at schools, colleges and the workplace. But building it has always been about getting the right humans on board. I believe that an entrepreneur's greatest strength is their ability to surround themselves with excellence. Your 'foil', your 'cornerstones', your 'dream team' – these are the people who will propel you to success, and it's all here in this book: how to find them, how to motivate them.

Business is also about principles. Integrity is one of our core values at CENTURY Tech. As well as providing sound 'how to' advice, *Beermat* is a book with strong values. Like everything in the book, these are born out of experience, not theory – and as such, will keep you secure under pressure.

I'm especially happy to see a new edition coming out. While the basic *Beermat* models and principles are timeless, it has benefited from being put in the context of the current business environment, using Mike's and Chris's own experiences since the early editions, and those of entrepreneurs who are currently building their businesses.

I hope many people will read this book, and be inspired to succeed. Good luck to you all on what will most certainly be one of your best adventures!

Preface to the third edition

When *The Beermat Entrepreneur* first appeared in 2002 I had no idea that the book would still be talked about and selling in 2018. (OK, like all entrepreneurs, I dreamt it would be, but my inner realist told me that I should not expect such good fortune.) However here it is, a book that is still popular and which some people have honoured with the description 'classic'. Wow!

I've learnt a lot since then – much of it through mentoring. Since the first edition came out, I have mentored over a thousand aspiring entrepreneurs. They come from all walks of life. They have business ideas of all kinds. They have radically different levels of ambition. While this book is essentially for ambitious entrepreneurs seeking to build sizeable and lasting businesses, I hope there will be plenty in it for people with other, less all-consuming visions.

How well have the models in the original stood the test of time? Overall, really well. Most needed gentle refining. Only the ownership model had to change radically. My insistence that the teamwork necessary to build a successful business be reflected in equal shareholdings for five key players simply didn't reflect how things happen – though a little bit of me still wishes it did. What haven't changed in *any* way are the Beermat approach and ethos.

This approach, for which the pub beermat is a metaphor, highlights simplicity (you can't write reams of managementese on a little square of paperboard) and people (a pub is a convivial place). The second of these is particularly important. 'Beermat' is about taking people seriously: the people you work with (your team) and the people you work for (your customers). It means thinking deeply about customer experience, even if you are not a service business. It is not about the exclusive pursuit of shareholder value, especially short-term shareholder value, to the detriment of all other considerations. It is, of course, about building great, highly profitable businesses. The ethos, which I describe in detail later, follows from this.

The shape of the book hasn't needed to change, either. I take the reader through the various stages of the enterprise's life, from that first moment where an idea emerges to the potential big sale at the end – while always aware that many great businesses find happy and profitable stopping points somewhere along this journey. There are three such stages, and there is a section of the book for each.

There are many people to thank for their input into the original and into this new version of *The Beermat Entrepreneur.*

First, Chris West, my friend and foil for nearly fifty years. Once again, he has accurately captured my content and voice, turning random content into a precise, logical model and producing another beautifully written book.

Tony Taylor has been my friend for nearly as long, and has provided both moral and financial support to the Beermat project since day one.

And also thanks to . . . Graham Michelli, for being a good friend to both Chris and myself for many years, for his input to the Beermat model and for allowing me to test the Sales on a Beermat material at international schools in exotic locations. Tony Heywood, for his tireless efforts in turning what we created into an online platform. Simon Graham and Nick Saalfeld for continuing support: running the Beermat Monday networking events, and their fine web work, podcast creation and written content. James Iyengar and Graham Dearing for helping me put all the unshapen entrepreneurial chaos into regular form and peaceful existence. Martin Rich and Erik Larsen at Cass Business School for giving me the platform to present the lectures that turned into the original version. Jim White from the *Daily Telegraph* and Jonathan Moules at the *Financial Times* for teaching me how to write newspaper columns. Roger Hamilton and Michelle Clarke for Wealth Dynamics, Talent Dynamics and all the fun we had in Bali. Robert Steinhouse for being a fine coach when I really needed it. Neil Mullarkey for teaching me how to improvise and to listen. John Lloyd for showing me how to be Quite Interesting. Andrew Grant and Caroline Wheller from

Aylesbury Vale District Council for boldly implementing the Beermat model in a local authority. Stephen King and Jeff Macklin for their insights into SME finance. Chris Spurgeon for his Virtual Finance Director work for both myself and my business over many years. Tony Waller from CMS and Dan Hall from Investec Wealth and Management for their expertise (and supporting all those excellent networking dinners). Kitty Underhill and Rachel Karn for advice on social media and on GDPR compliance. Roag Best for insights from a very different angle: the story of The Beatles.

Special thanks, of course, to Mike Banahan, Andy Rutter, Pete Griffiths and David Griffiths, for getting me started as an entrepreneur at The Instruction Set: I was previously selling scaffolding. To Bill Thompson for coming up with the title *The Beermat Entrepreneur.* To all the mentees I have met since 2002. I have learned considerably more from all of them than they ever did from me. Thanks to the team at Pearson for their work on the various editions, especially Rachel Stock for her enthusiasm for the first edition, Eloise Cook for seizing the baton and running with this new one, and Melanie Carter, Priyadharshini Dhanagopal and Suzanne Pattinson for editorial support. Thanks to Priya Lakhani for her fine foreword to this new edition.

For this rewrite we interviewed a small group of active entrepreneurs who shared their experiences with me. They may not be household names, but they are superb businesspeople who have built, or are building, great brands and companies. I found their input hugely enlightening and am massively grateful to them. (In case anyone asks, nobody paid to be in the book. I chose people I knew, liked and trusted and who felt the same about me – the Beermat way of doing things.) Thank you, Martin Dawson, Monique Drummond, Emma Killilea, Rupert Lee-Browne, Angela Middleton, Juliet Price, Steve Sampson, Harry Thuillier and Ian Walker.

Most important of all, I would like to thank my wife Virginia, another great foil, for all her love and support, without which I would probably still be gigging in pubs.

I am always delighted to get comments from readers. Is there anything we have missed? What's *your* experience of founding and building a business? Can I help with any current business problems? Please get in touch with me at mike@mikesouthon.com.

Mike Southon
London, May 2018

Publisher's acknowledgements

We are grateful to the following for permission to use copyright material:

Interview on page 71 courtesy of Harry N Thuillier, Co-Founder, Oppo Ice Cream & Desserts.

Once upon a time . . .

. . . there were three people sitting in a pub.

These three people talked, as people in pubs should do, about their enthusiasms. Some young men at the bar were discussing football. Two tables away, a young couple were discussing holding a housewarming party in their new home. Next to us, an older couple discussed the problem of moss on lawns. We were talking about business.

One of us had this brilliant idea – but he was always having brilliant ideas. But for once, his idea sounded special. Maybe this *would* work . . . I got another round in, and we began to look at the idea more closely, making notes on the beermats that were on the table, as we had no paper to hand.

Five years later, our company, The Instruction Set, was employing 150 people. Soon after that, it was sold, and we were millionaires.

After my earn-out period, I retired. Six months later, I started another business. It wasn't a 'failure', but it never really flew. Right now, I'm delighted it didn't, as I learnt almost as much from its shortcomings as I did from my success. I then joined another entrepreneurial team to help build a software company, which became worth over $1 bn. Sadly, I didn't get any stock options, but it paid the bills and was fun. I then worked in an incubator for a while – another invaluable source of learning. Then I sat down with Chris and we wrote *The Beermat Entrepreneur.*

Part of the above took place during that weird era of the late 1990s and the year 2000, the dotcom boom/bust, which was a giant lesson in how not to do business. After that, we kidded ourselves that those lessons had been learnt. However, they hadn't. That era's broken business model seems to keep on being reinvented, like a recurring nightmare.

> ### The dotcom era model of business development
>
> - Come up with a clever-sounding idea, based on whatever technology is in vogue at the moment
> - Draw a 'hockey-stick' graph showing all the money that will roll in as the business captures an ever-increasing percentage share of some huge market
> - Misquote the movie *Field of Dreams*, saying that if we build the business 'they' will come
> - Get people with more money than sense to throw millions of pounds at it
> - Headhunt, in a great panic, any skills you suddenly find you need
> - Misquote *Field of Dreams* again, to reassure everyone
> - Actually sell something to somebody (optional)
> - Get the hell out as quickly as possible, via an IPO if you can manage it, before the flaws in the idea become obvious

It didn't work at the turn of the millennium; it isn't working now.

By contrast, this book is about how to really make a business grow.

Business is simple

When I say that, it annoys some people. But it's true. Almost all the business disasters I have seen, and I've seen plenty, have been due to people getting very simple things wrong.

Simple doesn't mean easy. Success in business involves *hard work*. Lots of it, twenty-hours-a-day-for-five-years hard work. However, if you love business, you're up for that. With the right people and the right motivation, you'll enjoy it most of the time (not *all* the time – business is not that simple).

Note the caveat 'if you love business'. If you don't get a buzz from business – the ideas, the technology, the people – you really shouldn't go near a start-up. Or any commercial organisation, really. Scale down your financial ambitions and find another way of making both a living and a difference to the world.

Business also involves making *hard choices* – not often, but occasionally. However, these choices are often not as hard as they look. You know in your heart what you have to do; it's just a matter of summoning up the willpower.

Success also requires a measure of *luck* – but as the golfer Gary Player said, 'The harder I practice the luckier I get'.

However, I still believe that the biggest ingredient for business success is *following the right pattern.* This is what this book is about: a pattern that begins with self-examination and grows naturally from there, potentially to a point where you are leading an organisation that affects the lives of thousands of people: customers, employees, suppliers . . .

A successful business is a living thing. So like all living things, it has a natural pattern of growth. You ignore this at your peril, just as if you fail to re-pot seedlings at the right time they'll die, or if you plant a sapling in the wrong kind of soil you'll soon be confronted with a dead-looking stick instead of that riot of colour that you saw at the Garden Centre.

Some people balk at this talk of patterns. Isn't business about flair and imagination? Isn't business an art as much as a science? The great entrepreneurs didn't follow simple sets of rules, any more than Monet and Rembrandt went out and bought those kits where you dab paint into little numbered sections . . .

I can only say that the more I see businesses of all kinds fail or succeed, the more I believe that there is a pattern to their growth that has to be worked with to ensure success, and that I understand this pattern well enough to start telling other people about it.

There is, perhaps, an analogy with the way that scriptwriting is taught in Hollywood. There are strict rules for developing plots, rules that compel attention and that make stories work. But they do not of themselves guarantee success. If they are followed without flair, the results are leaden, and they end up with 'one star' on daytime TV. You need aptitude *as well as* rules to excel.

Which is why you must begin your journey to business success by asking . . .

Where do I fit in?

The popular vision of a growing company is of a group of followers flocking round the banner of a charismatic entrepreneur. The reality is much subtler than this. Yes, there will no doubt be an Oprah or a Branson at the centre of things, but they are not the whole story. There are concentric rings of very special people around every entrepreneur, without whom the business will go nowhere, and without whom the entrepreneur is more likely to spend their days tinkering with prototypes or impressing people at parties. This book is for entrepreneurs but just as much for the people who form these essential concentric rings.

For any individual wanting to work in an entrepreneurial environment, the first question must be 'What role am I best suited to play?'

The entrepreneur

Entrepreneurs are, for all their faults (see below), very special people. Are you one? Look in this mirror and be honest: is the face staring back yours?

Entrepreneurs are *visionary.* Most of us see things as they are, accept them and try and work around them. Entrepreneurs are different. They are mismatchers, rebels, people who see big opportunities that the rest of us miss. Having seen it, they cling to their vision and don't let anyone knock it down. Dreams 'fly forgotten' when the alarm goes and we have to get up; entrepreneurial visions stick around.

Entrepreneurs don't just see things differently and keep seeing them that way – they act on what they have envisioned. They are *doers,* people who delight in action.

They are *battlers,* too. I was going to say 'fighters', but that conjures up images of drunks picking fights. Entrepreneurs won't take 'no' for an answer. Barriers, difficulties and setbacks are challenges, to be risen to and pushed aside or worked around. This feistiness will be tested to the limit. Almost every successful entrepreneur I know has at least one story of when their business seemed doomed, but they found a way of saving it, whatever it took.

A common perception is that entrepreneurs are greedy. Many certainly want to make money, but I have met few for whom this is the main motivation. Instead, their vision becomes a *passion.* The business becomes an object of a kind of love, like an artist has for their creation or even a parent for their child. That's a much deeper driver than money. Several entrepreneurs have told me: 'Money is just how you keep the score.'

Entrepreneurs are *confident.* They are born optimists. This optimism is often irrational – it can infuriate their more realistic friends – but it just bubbles up in them. 'I can do it!' And, of course, they do.

Entrepreneurs are *charismatic.* Not just optimists, they have optimism to spare, optimism which they radiate and instil into others around them. No wonder they attract people, not just followers but energetic, imaginative winners. They'll need this quality, over and over again – with their business partners, with their employees, with their sources of finance, and most important of all, with their customers. But that's fine as they've got a seemingly endless supply of it.

There may appear to be exceptions to this: introvert business-builders who seem grey at first sight. However, my experience is that these people have a hidden charisma which they unveil in the right circumstances. Bill Gates, for example, is often parodied as being utterly uncharismatic, but I saw him years ago among a group of technical people, and he was the centre of attention.

Entrepreneurs are *in a hurry.* Not only are they going to change things, they are going to do it fast.

Luckily, they have bags of *energy.* They're going to need it, every ounce of it. But somehow, they know it's there. All the entrepreneurs I have met seem to sleep less than normal.

Their extra hours are filled with *hard work,* of course. Entrepreneurs, in love with their business, can become obsessed with work. When they're not doing it, they're talking about it. Not the best thing at dinner parties, but great for success.

Does this look like you? If so, be proud!

The Beermat guide to entrepreneur traits

- Visionary
- 'Doers' – love action
- Battlers – won't take 'no' for an answer
- Passion for the business
- Confident
- Charismatic
- In a hurry
- Lots of energy
- Hard work

Now for the difficult bit.

Entrepreneurs are also *arrogant*. They know they are good. At everything. With a strong team around them – and they can't flourish without such a team – this attitude mellows to 'I'm good at everything but I don't have the time to do everything, so I have to let the people in finance, sales, delivery (and so on) get on with it.'

But even then, the team needs to remain on guard against the entrepreneur's passion for meddling. The worst thing about this meddling is that it is appallingly inconsistent. One day the entrepreneur will be stomping round the office fixing light bulbs, the next phoning up customers out of the blue, the next trying to rewrite software, the next . . .

This arrogance is the 'flip' side of the entrepreneur's confidence and vision. Vision is not always a good trait: Hitler, Mao and Stalin knew they were right. But so did Winston Churchill, Mother Teresa and Nelson Mandela.

They are also *manipulative*. Just as arrogance is the flip side of the entrepreneur's confidence and vision, manipulation is the dark side of charisma. Entrepreneurs can use people. They may inspire them, they may enable them to achieve things they'd never achieve on their own, but they still use people.

That valiant refusal to take 'no' for an answer can easily morph into *pig-headedness.*

Entrepreneurial energy can often dissipate. They're forever coming up with new ideas. They love brainstorming sessions and blaze with excitement at new projects. 'Why don't we . . . ?' 'Supposing . . . ' 'And then we can . . . ' This is perhaps part of a bigger weakness, *lack of focus.* I said that entrepreneurs are obsessed with work, and they are. Yet at the same time many of them seem unable to focus on specific issues for any length of time. It's as if, having walled themselves away from most of what the rest of us call life, they have to pace round and round this little courtyard with extra energy. If you are an entrepreneur, please make yourself focus on detail. More important still, listen to your closest colleagues when they focus on detail.

Entrepreneurs can become *obsessed with the competition.* I know one who founded a company with the sole purpose of putting a rival out of business. I shall talk about 'how to compete' in the next chapter, but I don't think I'm giving too much away by saying this obsession can be disastrous, both commercially and personally. If you feel yourself going down this road – back off. Concentrate on improving *your* proposition.

Entrepreneurs can be *impatient.* They want everything done yesterday. Time is a precious commodity in business, so this is understandable, but sometimes you have to take things slow and steady, and entrepreneurs are often not good at this.

Oh, and . . .

- Arrogant
- Manipulative
- Pig-headed
- Lacking focus
- Obsessed with competition
- Impatient

So there we have it. Laid back, sophisticated, gentle? No. Contrary, childlike, obsessive – that's more like it. More like you?

I have come in for criticism for type-casting entrepreneurs in this way, but I stick to my guns. It fits the vast majority of the entrepreneurs that I have met. Obviously not every entrepreneur has all these strengths and all these weaknesses in full measure, but almost all of them have a healthy – and unhealthy – dose of them. The idea, popular in some business schools, that entrepreneurship is simply a set of behaviours that can be learnt by anyone does not fit with my experience.

This does not mean that learning the craft is an optional extra. People blessed with these traits are in pole position in the 'Entrepreneurship Grand Prix', but the race still has to be driven and won, with skill as well as passion.

Successful entrepreneurs create employment, opportunities, choice, wealth and change. They inspire people to do things of which they hardly imagined themselves capable. They challenge orthodoxy and convention, even when it is deeply entrenched in society and its institutions. They do this much more than most politicians. If it weren't for these men and women of vision, action and drive – with all their weaknesses – we'd probably still be sitting around in caves, chewing on our staple diet of mammoth. Entrepreneurs truly change the world.

But they don't do so alone.

. . . and their teams

I've had enjoyable debates with successful solo entrepreneurs, who say this is not the case. They gesture round at an open-plan office full of busy, engaged people and say that they built all this on their own. However, most of them turn out to be much better team-builders than they give themselves credit for. They have a natural talent for picking good people to work alongside them and for keeping such individuals motivated.

I also hear many stories of solo entrepreneurs who, rather than build teams, employ unconfident people whom they then bully. Usually, the underlings put up with this for a while then leave, after which the business implodes, leaving the entrepreneur ranting at the fickleness of humanity (apart from them), how they were let down by x, y and z (and so on). Of course, there are no absolutes: some of these 'my way or the highway' types do manage to build successful businesses. But that's not the Beermat way.

Beermat entrepreneurs build a team around them. Actually they build four teams, radiating out from them as the business grows: a foil, a founding team, what I call their 'dream team' and, finally, more conventional types of employee. These form at different stages of the growth of the business.

The foil

The foil is the first person the entrepreneur hooks up with, and usually the most important. Many great businesses are founded by an 'entrepreneur and foil' team. Many good businesses stumble or even fall when the entrepreneur and foil fall out.

Many entrepreneurs and foils were friends before the business begins. Some are actually siblings. The Instruction Set was an example of one of the latter (Pete and Dave Griffiths). Oppo Ice Cream (Charlie and Harry Thuillier) is another. Broker's Gin was founded by Martin and Andy Dawson. Other entrepreneurs struggle until they find the right foil. Monique Drummond of Relish Research says that her biggest break was not some giant piece of business but finding the right person to work alongside her to build the company.

Foils complement entrepreneurs. This can mean doing things that entrepreneurs don't get round to: completing (or quietly dropping) things that entrepreneurs have started but lost interest in; focusing on detail; unruffling feathers. It also means doing things from the start that the entrepreneur doesn't like doing (exactly what I shall explain below). It also means getting on with the entrepreneur, who can be moody. The ideal relationship between entrepreneur and foil is one of mutual trust and respect. Ideas can be discussed objectively. There's no 'point scoring', or if there is, the point scorer soon realises their mistake and makes amends. Criticism, and reaction to criticism, are not taken personally (for long, anyway).

Foils are also enthusiasts, of course, with almost as much passion for the business as the entrepreneur – nobody will quite love it the way the entrepreneur does.

The foil should be a different *personality type* to the entrepreneur. I don't want to go overboard on personality types, as it risks putting human beings, who are all delightfully different, into simplistic boxes. However, a little gentle, not-taking-it-*too*-seriously putting in boxes can be enormously helpful in making sense of the personality clashes often found in start-ups, and of the personality needs of start-ups. I find the following model simple but powerful.

Magnets are the charmers, the 'people people', the ones who have to be out there making new friends or introducing a to b. They have charisma. They impress. Magnets love the limelight, and somewhere deep inside they believe they have a right to be in it. In the less pleasant magnets, this belief has a sharp edge to it, a potentially fragile sense of entitlement. To the more pleasant ones, it's simply there. 'Why not? Someone has to be centre stage, so it might as well be me.' No surprises: sales people are magnets. Most (but not all) entrepreneurs fit into this category too.

Makers are the technicians, the designers, the system-builders, the architects. Apparently modest, they actually have a fierce pride in what they do. They love technical discussions. They do not love criticism of their work, except when it is a) very tactful or b) from someone whose expertise they are in awe of. They get enough criticism from themselves, anyway.

Monitors are the protectors. They are the members of old-fashioned 'professions'. Safety is paramount for them and lies in following correct processes and procedures. Many lawyers and accountants are monitors (though a savvy magnet who has mastered these skills can be *very* successful in business). Many HR people are monitors. I suspect all health and safety inspectors are.

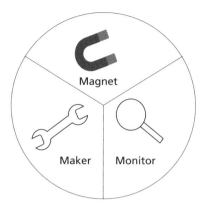

Magnets tend to be more outward-looking than makers or monitors, who are, instead, focused on themselves and the task they are engaged in. Magnets also tend to want to be liked, while makers and monitors will be happier to be judged by their work. They don't care what people think of them, as long as they know, inside, that they have done a good job.

Makers and monitors can fall into the 'perfectionist' trap of believing that if they create the perfect (by their own standards) product or the perfect system, the business will automatically prosper. Magnet perfectionism can go the opposite way, and try and overplease others, promising benefits way beyond what is actually possible.

Yes, almost everybody has a bit of each of these three types in them. But for most of us one of the three is dominant, and in some people – often the ones who excel in what they do – one is extremely dominant. Most monitors or makers can find their 'inner magnet' if they have to. Chris, my co-author, is a classic maker, but can be very sociable when he has to be. But most monitors or makers usually can't wait to get back to their preferred way of being and find it stressful to be asked to spend too long outside it.

If you're a devotee of the popular Myers-Briggs model, magnets tend to be ESTP/ENTP, makers ISTP and monitors ISTJ. But don't get too concerned if you did a Myers-Briggs test and didn't come out as one of these. Just ask 'Am I a magnet, a maker or a monitor?'

Returning to the subject of the foil, most entrepreneurs are magnets and for them the foil should be a maker.

However, some entrepreneurs are makers. This may sound odd, given my views on entrepreneur traits above, but it's true. Less common still, but often very successful, are 'monitor' entrepreneurs. The builders of large, now old-fashioned conglomerates like Hanson Trust, BTR, ITT and, going back even further, Standard Oil, fell into this category.

The 'maker' entrepreneur needs a 'magnet' foil, who will enjoy getting out there and engaging people in the project. There are plenty of examples of magnet foils, especially in the world of online enterprise, where maker entrepreneurs build and refine amazing systems and someone else does the communication. An outgoing individual with some experience in sales would be perfect for this role.

So who does the finance? In many start-ups, the answer is 'no one'. The maker should probably do the basic accounting, but the best answer is to pay a part-time, 'monitor' bookkeeper as soon as possible. Start-ups that require lots of cash to get off the ground will need not just a bookkeeper but a fully-fledged finance director from the beginning (they can be part-time too, but must be good), as someone needs to inspire investors with the belief that their investment will be monitored. But most start-ups don't need that much upfront investment (more on this below).

Problems arise when two makers form a team. One may be a bit more outgoing than the other, but such pairs often both secretly prefer building things and, in their hearts, believe that if they build them well enough, customers will come. In this case, a team of two makers, the more extrovert of them *has* to put down their tools or switch off their computer and become the salesperson. Or, the best strategy, they must both stop making things for a moment and concentrate on finding a magnet to join the team. I talk more about how they actually do this in the next chapter.

Less common is two magnets teaming up. Try pushing two actual magnets with the same polarity together and you'll see why. And if you do get two magnet individuals working together and working well, the immediate question arises: what exactly are they going to sell? Or, if they do create something saleable, who is actually going to buckle down and deliver it?

As a mentor, I meet many more makers than magnets or monitors. 'Find someone to sell it' is the piece of mentoring advice that I give most often.

The third person

It happens a lot: an entrepreneur and a foil have got a business up and running, but then they hit a wall of some kind. This is often in the form of a delivery bottleneck. The orders have started coming in faster than expected (often for no reason anyone quite understands) and suddenly the delivery schedules are slipping. The third person is someone who will sort this out, an experienced project manager or a bright, orderly-minded friend who picks this skill up very quickly. Such a person could well be a monitor, with the monitor's belief in the redemptive power of process, thus making up a powerful combination of magnet/maker/monitor in the business.

If the original pair consisted of two makers, the block will probably be shortage of sales. As I said above, the third person here needs to be a magnet.

The third full team member could be a finance specialist. However, my experience is that, for businesses where the finances aren't that complicated, the third person will usually be needed to beef up delivery or sales.

The arrival of a third person in the team can be disruptive for the entrepreneur and foil. I often draw the analogy of a marriage plus an outsider. But wise entrepreneurs and foils realise that some measure of disruption is needed if they are to build a business.

Cornerstones

These three people may end up as the *founding team* and run the show.

However, building a successful business involves so many different and crucial tasks that it is hard for three people to cover all the bases. I still prefer the next odd number up, five, to lead a growing business. (Odd numbers are best because that avoids stalemates in decision-making. A team of four can so easily fall into two camps of two each.) A top team of entrepreneur plus four *cornerstones*.

Three cornerstones will be in charge of the three essential tasks in a Beermat business: sales, finance and delivery. A fourth cornerstone brings a fourth skill, which varies from business to business. I call this the 'critical factor'. In technology businesses, this skill can be innovation. In consumer businesses it can be marketing (I shall say more about the critical factor cornerstone later).

The foil will usually end up playing one of the cornerstone roles. In The Instruction Set, Dave was foil to Pete, his entrepreneur brother, yet his formal title was finance director. He was our finance cornerstone (and an outstanding one). This looks like a demotion for the foil, who now appears to be just another member of the team of four around the entrepreneur. But it is best seen as an extra role for the foil, in response to the rising level of challenge created by the success of the business. The foil now has to wear two hats. Day to day, they take a back seat (albeit one in the boardroom). But, especially at times of crisis, they will have the entrepreneur's ear in a way that the rest of the top team never have. When we sold The Instruction Set, for example, the deal was organised by Pete and Dave, entrepreneur and foil.

It's a subtle balance.

I accept that many successful businesses don't have the five-person top team I advocate. Fine. There's almost always one entrepreneur, usually plus a foil. If they have any sense, they have a small number of highly reliable people supporting them, in charge of the key functions of the business. Whether they have boardroom authority or not – I believe they should have – these people are still the cornerstones on which the business is built.

I still recommend a top team of five if a business is to grow beyond the 25-people level. So if you are setting out to conquer the world, I suggest thinking about your foil and three other cornerstones from the very start. If you are less ambitious and thinking more along the lines of 'I want to start a business and see how far I can grow it, and if I end up with 25 people and a turnover of a few million pounds a year, I shall be deliriously happy', then a smaller team may well do.

Cornerstones, like foils, are very special people, with a magical mixture of solidity and entrepreneurial passion.

Their solidity comes from their *character.* They are reliable, conscientious, loyal.

It also comes from their commercial or technical *skills.* Cornerstones are professionals. In some start-ups, they may not be hugely experienced professionals, but they are hell-bent on mastering their profession. This provides essential objectivity.

Yet at the same time, they are *passionate* about the business. This is not just a dry exercise in expertise.

Cornerstones have considerable *personal skills.* It's not enough just to be reliable, good at a business discipline and passionate about the idea. Working with the mercurial entrepreneur, cornerstones need to be able to tell the truth tactfully, and to remain calm and cool when the entrepreneur still tries to overrule them.

They need the entrepreneur's capacity for *hard work* – there are no free rides in a new business. Cornerstones must have the same level of ambition as the entrepreneur and the foil. It can often happen that people say they are ambitious, but when the level of work needed to fulfil those ambitions become apparent, they realise that, actually, they have other priorities. No initial deception was involved – they just didn't know how strenuous it would be.

They need *courage,* possibly more courage than the entrepreneur at times. Entrepreneurs can be blinkered by their natural optimism, while cornerstones can see the potential hazards much more clearly.

A big ego can be a help to an entrepreneur, but not to a cornerstone. You've got to have *a bit of ego* to seize the leadership challenge that the cornerstone role involves. But not too much. In the end, the entrepreneur is the boss, and you must accept that.

The Beermat guide to cornerstone attributes

- Reliable
- Professional skills
- Passionate
- Personal skills
- Hard work
- Courage
- Moderate ego

Though cornerstones share these traits, it's important to note that in other ways they differ. Going back to our model of personality types, there needs to be a balance of magnets, makers and monitors in the top team. It is a mistake that some entrepreneurs make, to fill the business with people like themselves. In some ways they are right to – everyone in a start-up needs passion, commitment and adventurousness. But in other ways, the wise business builder looks for people of different temperaments, values those differences, and learns how to get the best from them.

You don't have to be a cut-out 'business type' to do well in enterprise. You have to be eager for the start-up adventure, but beyond that, you have to be who you are, play to your strengths and find an environment where that is what other people want from you. You should respect other people's different strengths too.

The dream team

When this top team starts hiring, a new, outer ring of special individuals will join the business – I call them the *dream team*, an analogy with sport.

Like cornerstones, the dream team's members are a mixture of conventional skills and entrepreneurial flair. Unlike the foil and cornerstones, they have less 'skin in the game'. They will have a lower level of skill and experience too. Much lower in the case of some dream-teamers, who may well be youngsters new to the world of work, with few formal skills. But they have bags of creativity and can-do spirit, and the start-up gives them the chance to express this. I shall say more about these wonderful people in the chapter on the 'sapling' enterprise.

Big company employees

This fourth, outer ring only develops if the company gets beyond a certain size. I shall talk about them in Chapter 4: The mighty oak.

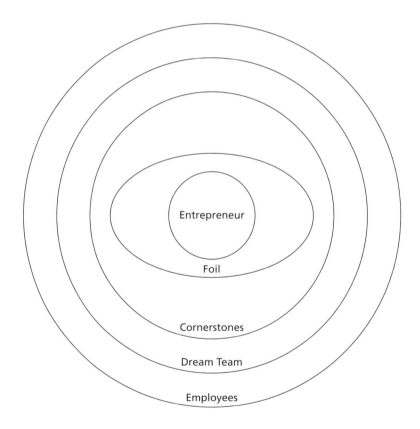

The entrepreneur and their teams

The intrapreneur

Do you work for a big company but secretly dream of being an entrepreneur? Do you at the same time fear the loss of security that would come from packing the job in and going it alone? I have met plenty of people in this situation. The way forward is to become an intrapreneur, initiating and driving new projects within the company.

Intrapreneurs have some advantages over the external start-up. Their employer may provide things such as premises, funding, marketing support, mentoring, contacts and access to a pool of talented potential cornerstones and a dream team, all of which the entrepreneur 'out there' has to go out and find. In return, of course, the intrapreneur loses freedom and the chance to become seriously rich. But many people find the compromise satisfying.

When *The Beermat Entrepreneur* first came out, intrapreneurship was frowned on in most companies (with a few notable exceptions). It was seen as unnecessarily 'rocking the boat'. Since then, more and more organisations have understood that intrapreneurs can be powerful sources of competitive advantage. Many now have formal systems whereby employees can submit entrepreneurial ideas to a panel, and, if they succeed, be given paid time, a budget, people and other resources to develop these ideas.

Some even have specific intrapreneurial divisions, where large, speculative projects are developed. The most notable is probably Google X, the company's skunkworks set up to invent and build 'moonshot' technologies, ones that it hopes will 'make the world a radically better place'. This has produced (amongst other things) the Waymo driverless car and Google Glass, the 'computer in a pair of spectacles'. X has recently been partially spun off from the parent organisation – it and Google are now both subsidiaries of Alphabet, a holding company – but it is still culturally a Google business.

The original skunkworks, by the way, was created by Lockheed Corporation during World War Two to design and build the US Air Force's first jet fighter, the P-80. The new division was located in a circus tent, next to an evil-smelling plastics factory which is how the skunkworks got its name. In those back-to-basics conditions, designers and engineers took a mere 143 days to design and build a working prototype. Such is the benefit of unleashing intrapreneurial energy.

Other companies, keen to hold on to talent, allow employees to take some time off to work on their own 'side hustles'. This seems particularly common in the media world.

Sadly, however, many companies still don't value intrapreneurship, and this can make life tough for the entrepreneurially minded employee. If your current employer is dead set against such subversive radicalism, it's time to look for somewhere where your imagination and energy will be valued and put to use.

The fundamental process of building an enterprise is the same within a company as outside it, so intrapreneurs should read this book and follow it as closely as entrepreneurs in the world out there.

Note that for companies, letting intrapreneurs loose is not a pure win – there will be some downsides. Remember those negative attributes of entrepreneurs: you are just about to unleash these people (or at least gentler but still disruptive versions of them) on your tidy corporate culture. Some valuable, solid team players may be offended by their unconventional attitudes and buccaneering style. Of course, I think you've done the right thing – you're getting back to being a proper business again, not a Jurassic customer-proof bureaucracy. But watch out for a few internal bruises.

Your private life

Setting up and running a business is about as demanding an activity as you can get. If you are in a relationship it may not survive the competition. If you already have a family think very carefully about how you are going to balance your time.

Entrepreneurs (and foils and cornerstones) often tell their long-suffering partners: 'I'm doing this to give us a good life.' This is at best a half-truth. You're doing this because you need to, somewhere deep within you. Money is only a part of the reward. The partners of entrepreneurs may well feel jealous of their passion for the business. I don't blame anyone who feels this.

It takes a special person to partner an entrepreneur, foil or cornerstone. They have to be calm and not too dependent. A life of their own will protect them from their partner's crazy schedule: early starts, late home, sudden meetings or jumping on a plane to meet an overseas customer or technical expert. They have to be interested in the business as they'll hear a lot about it over the breakfast table – assuming their partner is at breakfast rather than having already been at work for two hours. The best ones know their partner so well that they can tell when that line between hard work and destructive stress has been crossed, and can choose a good time, sit them down and get them to open up about it.

Female entrepreneurs, foils or cornerstones can be faced with a problem here, as some men still find playing a supporting role difficult. In the 21st century they shouldn't. If a man is giving maximum support to his partner as she builds a great business, he should be hugely proud of both himself and her. But not every bloke has reached this point. If you love someone who is not really good at this stuff, find a support network that will provide it.

Some people, of course, find themselves single, or prefer so to be, or have a same-sex partner, or have multiple partners . . . Whatever your situation or choice, if you are entrepreneur, foil or cornerstone you will need support on a personal level. Make sure you get it.

The worst kind of partner for an entrepreneur is one who sees them as a ticket to a good life. That's OK, I suppose, if the business succeeds, though not something I have any respect for. But if the business tanks, which it is more likely to if the entrepreneur is poorly supported emotionally, then watch this kind of person stalk off in high dudgeon at their entitlement to wealth having been disappointed, probably blaming you for failing them in some way.

It might sound a bit corny, but the truth is that the best partner for an entrepreneur is one who loves them and who is loved back. But even the most loved-up couples should talk the issues through in advance. And keep talking.

> ## The Beermat entrepreneur's perfect life partner
>
> - Calm
> - Not too dependent
> - Accepts the crazy hours
> - Interested in the business
> - Can get them to talk
> - ♥♥!

Business can put a strain on relationships through time away from home and the company of glamorous, interesting (and often, underneath it all, insecure) people. If you sense a confession coming up – sorry, I was single during my time as a cornerstone and stayed that way. This was more due to pressure of work than any choice. I remember going on a date with a lovely woman, who seemed to find me attractive too – and falling asleep over dinner, because I'd been so busy at work. She was very understanding. I met my future wife after selling the business, when I had time to conduct a relationship properly.

If you have kids, then the issue gets more serious still. I'm not saying don't get involved in an ambitious start-up – and if I were to, and you were a natural entrepreneur, you wouldn't listen anyway – but work this out. Talk, talk, talk.

You can forget that much-loved hobby, of course – for the moment, anyway. Later on, you may be able to enjoy it extravagantly.

Of course, some couples do things differently, and actually either *both* run the business or have it so one of them plays a role in a business that the other runs. This is an impressive achievement.

There's an interesting debate about the best time in your life to start a business. I'm not sure this debate is hugely productive as different people have different journeys. But I would advise anyone wanting to start straight from school or university to spend at least a couple of years in employment first. You'll learn a hell of a lot in that time. If you want to set up a business in a particular sector, get a job in it. If for some reason you can't, just get into the world of work anyway.

Taking this further, I like the idea of spending your early twenties trying various ways forward, then getting really good at one specialist thing in your late twenties and early thirties, and finally starting out on your own aged around 35. But I appreciate that not everyone will see things this way. Some of the ablest entrepreneurs I know, such as Martin and Andy Dawson, started much later than this, after quite long careers in corporate-land. Maybe the best advice is to start out when your gut instinct screams at you to. 'The time is now. I just know. It's a gut feeling . . . ' Lots of entrepreneurs have told me that, or something similar.

So you're ready to go – ready and hungry. And you were honest about yourself, so you really know what role suits you best. Entrepreneur? Foil? Cornerstone? Dream-team player? Intrapreneur?

Time to get moving!

The seedling enterprise

There are very different stages that a business passes through on its way to maturity. These stages are radically different from one another – in culture, people, management style, finance, selling. In everything really.

So different and distinct are these stages, that I nearly chose the metaphor of a butterfly, whose larval, pupal and free-flying phases are totally unrecognisable as being related to the same creature. But there is a little more continuity than this – and anyway, will the massive company you eventually build really resemble one of those beautiful but evanescent creatures that flaps across your garden on a summer's day (till the cat attacks it)?

I prefer the metaphor of an oak: beautiful, spreading, long-lasting. It starts life as a *seedling* (foresters define a seedling as any young tree below a metre in height), grows into a *sapling*, and finally becomes the *mighty oak*.

This chapter is about the time as a seedling. This is about getting established. Trees produce hundreds of seeds. Many of these seeds produce small shoots, but most of these shoots quickly fall victim to weather, competition or hungry herbivores. A few of them make it to the one metre mark.

The seedling business is essentially the founding team plus (as the business grows) various types of support it may bring in, such as the weekly bookkeeper and (later) the part-time FD, plus a small group of trusted advisers. As they grow towards their 'one metre', seedling service businesses may be taking on part-time staff to deliver their product.

The vast majority of businesses in the UK are seedlings. Some are on their way to something bigger, but many of them are happy to be small, and have no desire to grow further. The Beermat approach, ethos and models still apply to such businesses. You still need to love your business, to assemble a balanced team, to be liked by customers and prospects. There will be plenty in this book for you.

Of course, before even the tiniest seedling can force its way up into the daylight, a seed has to germinate . . .

A good idea

Where do the really good ideas come from, and how do you *know* which ones are good and which not so good?

Where do they come from?

In my view, the answer is personal experience. A salesperson knows their customers have been crying out for a widget that does X properly, but nobody's making a decent one at the moment. A technical expert is convinced that there's a way to write software that does Y (or that does good old Z much cheaper). A small business owner finds themselves in breach of a new set of health and safety regulations they didn't know existed. A consumer is fed up with the quality of items on offer in a particular area, or with the poor standard of service that goes with them.

I find it helpful to map these examples on to a matrix. I don't use matrices a lot, but sometimes they come in handy. 'Beermat' businesses fit on to this model.

Some semantic points. The matrix distinguishes between 'goods' and services, not 'products' and services. I prefer to use the word 'product' in its broadest sense, not as a thing but as 'a definable set of benefits that someone can buy'. A day's consultancy is a product – a 'service product' – if it sets out to deliver clear, definable benefits. If it fails to deliver them, it's still a product, but one that needs work. Some people may use other terms like 'offer' for a service product, and keep the word 'product' for goods, for things. Fine, as long as they set out clearly what they mean and stick to it. What matters is the consistent use of these sometimes slippery terms.

The matrix is not a static one. Clever 'goods' businesses can create extra value by moving along the horizontal axis and *adding service*. This is very Beermat. 'Can you add service?' is a great question to ask any goods entrepreneur trying to improve their products. Clever service providers can create bespoke goods to sell along with the service. Companies serving businesses can sometimes craft products for the public. A consumer product company can move up the vertical axis and start serving business customers. But most businesses have their heart, or at least their roots, in one of the boxes.

It's not an all-embracing model either. People make excellent money in things like property, and this doesn't fit on to the matrix anywhere (though even if you buy old properties, do them up and then sell them, you are adding value for the ultimate purchaser).

In all the boxes, a good business idea begins with a magic question: *'Where's the pain?'*

Business ideas which don't do anything about pain run the risk of becoming solutions in search of problems.

People used to marketing consumer goods may consider this question dull. Didn't the great campaigns add 'perceived value' to things by making them look more fun? But modern consumers are savvy. 'You don't really need this, but you'll love it' can be a creative sell, but it is risky. If you can find some kind of consumer pain, you have a more compelling offer.

Ed Bussey's Figleaves website solved the pain of people who wanted to buy lingerie but were either too busy or too embarrassed to walk into a shop and place an order.

Charlie and Harry Thuillier wanted to produce ice cream that we could enjoy without the nagging doubts of knowing that it's not very good for us.

Emma Killilea discovered she had coeliac disease in 2002. This meant she needed to remain on a gluten-free diet for the rest of her life. At that time, there was only a narrow range of poor substitutes available. She said she could do better than that, went to university to study food technology and started a business making gluten-free food. Delicious Alchemy now sells to all the major supermarkets, providing both own-label and branded products.

Ian Walker realised that ambitious, busy office workers in London didn't have time to organise their laundry. Laundry Republic takes care of it, collecting, cleaning to the highest standard and delivering it back.

For business customers, the big pains are money, time and effort. Probably in that order, though it will be different for different customers.

Money is certainly the easiest one to focus on, as once the idea is up and running, you can easily demonstrate its benefits. 'Our software saved XYZ Ltd £10,000 in its first month. Here's the story . . . ' You can't beat that.

If you can, find a way of lessening the customer's financial pain that isn't just by being cheaper (unless you have a radical, disruptive way of making your offer *a lot* cheaper). Price wars are hell, and play into the hands of large, established businesses with deep pockets. Can you save your customers' money by helping them do something better or more efficiently?

Time is harder to quantify, but you can have a go. 'Joanna Bloggs, owner of XYZ, reckons that our service saved her company 100 hours in its first month.'

Then it gets more difficult. *Effort* is often very difficult to translate into numbers, but people know it when they feel it. 'Our service removes all the pain of moving offices.' A subtler version of this is being *nicer* to deal with than the opposition, thus removing the pain of surly or unhelpful service. This can be a powerful sell over time, but it is difficult to convince people of this to begin with. Everyone starts out claiming they are nice to deal with.

A vaguer pain is *fear of missing out*. This is a real issue at the back of the minds of many business owners or managers. 'Is there some disruptive trend I don't know about, that rivals are already leaping on, and which will suddenly turn out to give them a huge competitive advantage and which will make us look like dinosaurs?'

Disruptive platforms can create great opportunities for enterprise. Think of all the enterprises that started up using sites like eBay (the customer pain here is often the difficulty of sourcing niche items at a sensible price). Remember that you don't have to create market disruption to benefit from it. For every eBay – or Airbnb, Amazon, Etsy, Redbubble or Uber – there are vast numbers of nimble, entrepreneurial businesses piggybacking on these platforms and flourishing.

The Beermat hierarchy of business pains

- Money
- Time
- Effort
- Dealing with unpleasant people
- Fear of missing out

Entrepreneurs are never short of ideas. If you are reading this and thinking that you'd like to run your own business but you can't think of what to do, you are not ready. Wait till you are seized by a furious determination to do or make something better than it's being done or made at the moment and an insight into how you really could make that happen.

Alternatively, check out franchise models, which will solve this problem for you. Choosing the right one can be tricky (and choosing the wrong one can be expensive), so do your research thoroughly.

If you do take out a franchise, keep this book by your side. Almost all of what it says about start-ups will apply to your business too.

How do you spot if a new idea is a winner?

The answer to this, sadly, is you can't. You can have a good feeling about it, but you only know the true mettle of an idea once you test it. People are always approaching me with ideas, asking what I think of them. My reply is always that I don't know. It sounds fine, but only paying customers can give a valid verdict.

What I can say is that there are a number of clear hurdles that the idea will have to jump.

The first one is simply there, in the pub. If the entrepreneur's friends light up and someone says 'Now that *is* a brilliant idea!' you have a small but real confirmation. Intuition is at work.

A second hurdle is the next morning when you wake up. In the clear light of day – and, depending on what was being consumed, of sobriety – is it really such a good idea?

You should have decided the night before to go away and do a little research on the idea. If you are potential cornerstones, you will do this – not because you read it in this book, but because your curiosity and professional pride will make you do so. If you're in sales or are a natural magnet, you'll at once start thinking of who you know who would be interested in it. If you're a designer, you'll knock up a prototype. If you are more into the nuts and bolts of making or delivering things, you will have thought about these processes, how they might work and what they might cost.

Gather again and compare notes. Are you still excited? Great. A third hurdle has been cleared.

Now is the time to draw up your first business plan. Unlike those business plans the size of blockbuster novels that some advisers tell you to write at this point, this plan is simple. So simple that you can write it down on the back of a beermat. It has three things on it, your elevator pitch, your first customer and your mentor.

I call this plan your original beermat. It is, in its quiet way, a hugely powerful business tool.

Your elevator pitch

The elevator pitch is what you would say about your business to your dream customer if you found yourself in an elevator with them (or in a lift, if you meet them in the UK). They get in on Floor 1 and press 6. You've then got the intervening floors to convince them of the value of your idea. I've heard, and still hear, too many so-called elevator pitches that assume the lift gets stuck half way. Please, if you are approaching me or anyone else with an elevator pitch, stick to the rules.

The Beermat elevator pitch is only three sentences long: the *pain*, the *premise* and the *proof*.

Pain

What is the pain and who feels it most strongly? Or, more subtly, who, among potential customers that you can easily reach, feels it most strongly?

Premise

What are you going to do about that pain?

I've worked with some great entrepreneurs with great elevator pitches. I've mentioned some consumer ones above. Here are some great business ones.

Angela Middleton wanted a recruitment agency that didn't just provide staff but helped them and their new employers develop their skills.

Graham Michelli wanted to provide international schools with a complete uniform service, not just selling the uniforms but advising on materials, dealing with any parental complaints and sorting any problems with customs.

Juliet Price wanted an HR consultancy that provided a full, in-house service with no associates or anonymous call centres.

And, of course, The Instruction Set provided training in what was then a radical new operating system that organisations suddenly needed to know about, backed by the expertise of the two leading UK experts on the subject.

Be inspired by these. Don't be put off, afraid that your idea won't be as good. Your elevator pitch does not have to be perfect at this early stage. It will grow and change as you develop it, probably the moment you start talking to potential customers and almost undoubtedly once you start working with real ones.

Proof

The job of the proof is to lend credibility to the premise and convince people who hear it that you can really deliver on what you claim. The classic British proof is 'By appointment to Her Majesty'. Good luck on achieving that. For now, a humbler endorser will have to do: someone who has used your offer and likes it.

That, obviously, will have to wait until you get customers – to begin with, can you get a personal recommendation from someone?

> ## The Beermat elevator pitch
> - Pain
> - Premise
> - Proof

It's time to start selling.

Your first customer

The next item on your original beermat is your first customer. Sitting there in the pub (or waking up next morning) you haven't got one – though I've seen an enthused magnet going up to a group of people in a pub and trying to get them interested in an idea, so maybe, just maybe, you have. You should have someone in mind. Possibly your idea arose from a conversation with someone you know would buy it (one of those 'If only I had an x that did y, I'd pay z for it' conversations that entrepreneurs dream of). But most likely, nobody's actually bought anything yet.

That needs to change as soon as possible.

Ideally, after that first session, someone in your team will have produced an informal list of potential prospects. Ideally, this will include friends of theirs, as well as just business contacts. You'll be meeting up again soon – very soon if you have the enthusiasm required of a founding team. At this second get-together ('meeting' is maybe still too formal a term), discuss this list and see if the rest of the team can add to it. Everybody has *some* contacts.

If nobody in your team has produced such a list, this is a flashing red warning signal (plus one of those irritating klaxon things) that your team is lopsided. You need a magnet, the charmer who will draw in business.

It's a common problem. How do you find one?

Top salespeople are used to earning large commissions. Unless you're very lucky you won't know someone like this well enough to persuade them to do some fun selling for you. Fun plus an amazing future if things take off, but you can't guarantee that at the moment. And even if you do find such a person and persuade them, not every big-hitting salesperson is right for selling new things.

There are essentially two types of salesperson. *Hunters* go out and get new business. *Farmers* work existing accounts, keeping clients happy and seeing if there is any other pain that needs solving. Many highly paid salespeople are farmers and are very good at it – hence their salary. But the start-up needs a hunter.

I suggest an alternative to getting in an old pro. Find someone with the appropriate character, get them enthused about the idea and tell them to learn to sell. Selling isn't like accountancy, with lots of concepts to master. The basic principles are very simple – I teach them in half a day on my '*Sales on a Beermat*' workshops. From then on, salespeople refine their craft by doing. So the right type of person can get on the road very quickly. They won't be a sales genius from day one, but with a good enough idea and the Beermat methodology, they can quickly begin doing their job well – and enjoy it.

Start with people you know, like and trust. If they are going to become a key member of your business team, they are going to be very important people in your life.

I became sales cornerstone of The Instruction Set because I was a competent, eager salesperson who happened to know the two technical wizards in the founding team. Not through business networking but because we had done a student revue at the Edinburgh fringe (one of them had been our van driver).

If nobody you know *well* fits the bill, brainstorm people you know *of* . . . What about Carl? What about Shona? What about, what's-her-name, that really cheerful woman who works in customer service? Think of old acquaintances at school or uni. Who was always founding societies or organising events? Who enjoyed matchmaking? Who *had* to have people around them?

When persuading this person to join the team, the best inducements are that they know, like and trust you and that they want to be part of your gang. That last bit might sound childish, but that passionate sense of belonging is one of the most enjoyable and motivating things about starting a business. I know someone who works at persuading young people from rough estates to quit real gangs and set up in business. The clever pay-off is that they can be in a gang after all, but one that provides people with things they want and makes money legitimately, rather than practises pointless violence.

The next best inducement is that they will enjoy the selling as they are 'people people'.

The promise of a stake in a business is a third inducement, but that is still a distant glow on the horizon. Make sure they understand that the promise is dependent on them doing their job superbly and on them gelling in as part of the team.

Some people, even despite these attractions, may still have reservations. Sadly, sales is still regarded by many as a rather sleazy occupation. Your bright magnet mate who's perfect for the job might have their eyes set on higher, 'professional' things – or think they have anyway.

Beermat selling is not about sleaziness. It's not about duping people into buying things they can't afford, don't need or don't even really want. It's about finding out what customers' pain is and helping them get rid of that pain. The sales cornerstone of a successful enterprise can take enormous pride in their achievement, which is just as great as that of the technological genius or visionary entrepreneur. The sales cornerstone is the one who makes it real, who turns a great idea in a pub into something that customers first know about and then come to love. If you had seen as many businesses fail through lack of a sales cornerstone as I have, you would realise what a magical and impressive achievement that is.

Once this objection has been overcome, the potential sales cornerstone may still be worried about the commitment involved. Make it easy for them. To start with, ask how much time they have spare and let them work with that.

A salesperson recruited this way may not have contacts in the business area you seek to serve. If none of the rest of you has either, don't despair. You may have to leap a stage and start building the 'sales funnel' described below. It's harder starting out that way, but you'll be doing that soon anyway. In the end, if your idea is good, if you are a good team and if you work hard and in a structured way, results will follow.

However most founding teams will be able to cobble together a few personal contacts. This is the place to start selling. If the contacts come from the salesperson, they should simply ring each contact and ask for 15 minutes of their time. If the contacts come from a technical or finance person, it can be a bit more complicated. If the contact is a very shy technical wizard, they are best first approached by a fellow technician, who can then sell them the idea of meeting the salesperson. My advice is to let whoever has the connection decide who makes the first call, as long as it is clearly understood that the aim is to get the salesperson in front of the contact as soon as possible.

At their *first meeting* with any prospect, the salesperson will be doing a lot more listening than talking – and *no selling*. They will not be passive, however. The skill is to say as little as possible, but at the same time direct the conversation where you need it to go: their business, its pains, how those pains are solved (or not) at the moment. Or, more bluntly, does the prospect have *needs* and *money today*?

- **Needs**: What exactly is the pain? How are they (or their organisation) solving it right now? In what ways is the current solution unsatisfactory?
- **Money**: People rarely volunteer this information, so there is one direct question that has to be asked at this first meeting: 'Do you

have a budget for solving this pain?' If the person doesn't know, they are probably not the right person to be talking to. But they may say they will let you know. Let them. Don't think it is rude or somehow inappropriate to ask this question. This is business. Don't ask it 30 seconds into the meeting, of course. Wait till you have understood the pain, expressed some empathy and generally set up a tone of 'Wouldn't it be nice to be rid of that pain?' Then ask.

- **Today**: Sometimes you get lucky. The prospect is really looking for a solution to the problem right now and tells you that your timing is excellent. Emma Killilea phoned a retailer for a catch-up chat and was asked to come and pitch the next day, as they had just fallen out with their existing supplier. This sounds like a fairy-tale, but remember the Gary Player quote. Keep plugging away, and you will get lucky if your idea is timely. If your timing isn't perfect, find out when the prospect will next be considering their solutions to the pain you can solve.

The magic trio

Does the prospect have:

- needs *and*
- money
- today?

During this meeting, watch out for *buying signals* – indications that the prospect is eager to buy. This may sound obvious, but I've often seen salespeople miss these, because they were too 'in their own head' and not paying proper attention to the prospect. These signals can be physiological – relaxed posture, eye-contact, a smile. They can be verbal. 'We really do need an x!' is the ideal one, but any discussion of the pain, and how much it is a nuisance, is good. Even objections to what you are suggesting can be positive. The prospect is running a movie in their head of using what you are offering, and the inevitable complications are springing to mind. All good movies have complications. Lead them past these.

At the end of the meeting, summarise what you think their needs are, and say you need to talk to the rest of the team and will get back to them within 24 hours. Don't try and sell anything. Then, of course, fulfil your promise. Get the team together. Talk through what you can do for the prospect, given their budget (assuming they have told you what that is). Then send an email restating your summary of what you thought their pain was, then saying what the team has agreed you should offer as a solution. Ask for another meeting. Suggest a date and time.

At this *second meeting* you will be selling – agreeing with the prospect what you will provide and asking for money for it. If it's a big sale, other meetings may be necessary, but try and get something sold as quickly as possible (the 'tiny thing', described in the section on the Beermat sales funnel further on in this chapter).

Don't offer free stuff. I know we are now in a freemium world, where everyone expects goods and services for nothing, but in my experience people still don't really value these free things, however useful they have been. You need to establish from day one that you are offering something of value.

What value? In your own mind, you should have some idea of what your idea is worth. Look round the market at the products most like yours. Be humble when you do this. Few business offers are actually as radical as the originators believe them to be. Who are your nearest rivals, what do they offer and how much do they charge for that?

But that's only a guideline. What *really* matters in pricing is how much the pain-removal is worth to the customer. So the more you know about your customer's business – not just roughly what they make and do, but the precise details of how they do it and at what cost – the better placed you are to guess the right price for what you are selling.

You can of course offer an early adopter discount – and deepen the discount for upfront payment. I'm against giving discounts (except for early payment) once you are established, unless business dries up or you hit a horrendous cashflow crisis, but here you can allow yourself this luxury.

Start-up pricing: the magic questions

- *Who* are our nearest rivals?
- *What* do they offer?
- *How* is it different from what we offer?
- *How much* do they charge?
- *How much* is the pain removal worth to the customer?
- *How much* early adopter discount can we sensibly offer?

At some point, if your idea is any good and if your salesperson has enough magnetism, someone will say they'll give it a go.

Result!

Deliver a brilliant product. If you can, do more than you promised. But only a little more, as doing too much sets a tone of not sticking to agreements and unnecessary rescuing.

When your first customer pays you real money, it's a very special moment. Savour it. Back when The Instruction Set was founded, people paid by cheque. Once our first cheque had been cleared, we got it back from the bank, framed it and hung it on our wall.

If you have a product that will take a long time to develop, it might seem like you have nothing to sell at the moment. But if you believe that there is a real pain out there and that you have the means of solving it, can you sell some kind of pain relief consultancy? 'We're working on something that will really sort this, but right now we can help you in more conventional ways.' This will get you noticed in the relevant market, and no doubt teach you more about the pain, how it is actually felt and what to do about it, all of which will feed into the creation of the long-term product on which you are working.

The customer case study

You've sold your idea, delivered it and the customer is satisfied. Better still, the customer is delighted. You did what you said you would do, apart from a few glitches which you went in and fixed straightaway at no extra cost.

The idea has just leapt over another hurdle. It has become a real product, not just a theoretical one. It's time to set out its exact nature and benefits – though remember that this is a working definition, not a final one. The nature and benefits will almost undoubtedly change over time. But this is what you've got now, and it's special. Pin it down!

Do this with a customer case study. Keep it short and snappy. Even if you are in a high-tech business that prefers long, complex White Papers, do this instead. (If the techies insist on a White Paper, do it as well.) The customer case study is the *story* of the sale. Like all good stories, it has a beginning, middle and end.

The *beginning* is the customer pain. Simple.

The *middle* is how you solved it. This may also be simple, but certainly with most new service offers there are usually complications. The pain wasn't caused exactly by the things the customer thought it was, or your offer didn't quite sort it properly and you had to improvise a little.

The *end* is a happy customer. Try and quantify their happiness, ideally in terms of money saved, or if not, time saved, or if not, hassle saved (see the hierarchy of pains above). Get a quote from them and ask their permission to use it in subsequent publicity. You now have an early proof that you can use in your elevator pitch.

Note that if the customer really loved you, you may be able to make them into what I call a 'customer mentor' – of which more later.

The case study is a marvellous sales and marketing tool. Clear it with the subject and then put it on your website. Make sure that *everyone* in the business knows it and can tell it to anyone who asks them who they work for. It is a simple story, so it can be related informally.

It is also a product development tool. I suggest writing two versions of the case study. One is for public consumption, and is upbeat and positive. The other is for the team only, about the lessons you have learnt from the delivery.

Subsequent sales

Your first sale was a great moment and you were right to celebrate it. But don't get carried away and start ramping up spending on marketing, premises and so on (I've seen people do this). Teach yourself to be cautious.

Your early sales and deliveries will all be learning experiences on a steep curve. Some aspects of the product won't work. Others will work better than expected. You will discover some totally new things you can offer or new ways of offering existing benefits. Many successful businesses have started out planning to solve one pain and ended up solving another one. We intended The Instruction Set to be a software developer with training as a sideline to bring in quick cash, and ended up with a company that made most of its money from training.

Picasso once said, 'To know what you're going to draw, you have to begin drawing.'

This is a big reason why 'old hands' at corporate sales often make poor sales cornerstones for start-ups. They are used to selling an existing product list. The Beermat start-up sales cornerstone is more a negotiator and even a product developer, eager to work with the customer on improving the offer.

At the same time, don't be led too far down long blind alleys by customers who aren't sure what they want and endlessly suggest changes. There's a subtle balancing act here. At some point, your delivery cornerstone has to say 'We think x is best. Trust us, we're the experts.'

Over time, unless you offer very bespoke consultancy where every gig is radically different, you will be looking to establish a suite of products. But don't rush into that. (More about this in the section on marketing in Chapter 3: The sapling enterprise.)

The flaky foil

I've found this a lot in mentoring. People come to me, talk a bit about some minor business issues, then confide that their real problem is that they have started up the enterprise with someone but that someone is no longer pulling their weight. What should they do?

The answer is 'act quickly'. It's time for ways to part. This can be very difficult if the foil is someone close to you, which many of the best foils are. But all the more important to get things sorted. Sit them down, buy them a drink and tell them that it's not working. Have examples to hand of things that have gone wrong.

If the flaky foil comes up with a really convincing story, and an even more convincing story of how they understand the problem and are going to remedy it, and a deadline by which they will do this, then it might be worth giving them another chance. But no more excuses!

Acting quickly, especially on signs of trouble, is a key entrepreneurial skill. Most of us initially react to trouble by hoping that we can somehow work our way round it. Successful entrepreneurs grab any dangerous-looking bulls by the horns as quickly as possible.

Friendship can suffer as a result of such a separation. Accept this. The new enmity may not last. The foil goes away, realises that they weren't pulling their weight, and reconnects.

If you split up with your flaky foil then try a new one and the same problems occur, then maybe it *is* the idea that's at fault. Talk to people.

However, most entrepreneurs I know will be unwilling to ditch their idea and will keep looking and looking for the right people to help them realise it. I think they are wise to do so, though not forever. Knowing when to finally abandon a cherished business idea is more a matter of intuition than any science. Makers in particular can cling on too long.

Chris knew a musician who worked on a synthesiser for years. He kept being leapfrogged by big corporations and never made any money from it. They have now lost touch: the guy may still be in his garden shed right now, just adding one more feature. Often with entrepreneurs the decision to quit gets made for them, when the money runs out or a better idea comes along.

However, I shall stay positive. Your first foil wasn't up to the job, but the new one is doing a great job. The business is moving ahead.

Making it official

For legal and tax reasons, but also because it shows seriousness of intent, you should consider becoming a private limited company (technically, a private company limited by shares) once you start having customers. Your business will then be called 'its name Limited' and can have 50 shareholders. You can remain a private limited company for ever, which can be an attractive course of action – see the comments about stock exchange listing in Chapter 4: The mighty oak.

The easiest way is to do your company registration yourself via the internet. If you prefer doing things person to person, ask a solicitor if they have a fixed price service whereby they will register you. You need to have a solicitor anyway – not because you are bound to meet legal obstacles but in case you do – so this is one way of testing one out.

Put some money into the business to cover basic start-up costs. It doesn't have to be much. More on funding later.

Take a little time to ponder your company name. It should be memorable. It should be appropriate to your customer group and should tell people what you do. Ideally, it should be available as a domain name (.com and .co.uk), though if it isn't, this isn't the end of the world. We've been very happy with beermat.biz. If you really can't think of a name, have an informal chat with someone in advertising, as these people often have a knack for thinking up snappy names. Or was there someone at school who always came up with catchy and probably not very flattering nicknames for people?

When you register a company, you become a company director. This means you are taking on certain legal responsibilities. I recommend a brief chat with your solicitor. Don't be scared off by this stuff, but be aware of it.

Who owns what?

In the original *The Beermat Entrepreneur* I said that the entrepreneur and the four cornerstones should split the equity five ways. I now realise this was idealistic. It's what we did at The Instruction Set and it worked. But in the 16 years since the book appeared, I've hardly met anyone else who has done the same.

Instead, I suggest that the founding team agree initially to split the equity between them as a temporary measure, but at a later date – set one, say in six months' time – they will sit down and have an *equity meeting*, a very grown-up discussion about how the equity should be more permanently split.

Remember that you don't have to hand out all the shares when you start. Your company can have 1,000 'authorised' shares, but if only three of those shares are apportioned, one to each member of the founding team, then each team member owns one third of the company.

As the business develops, it can happen that the founding team all put as much effort in, and all turn out to be as skilled as each other. Keep that three-way split.

More likely, however, is that some will find themselves putting more in than others. This isn't usually out of laziness, just priorities. Some people might have academic projects, family commitments, day jobs that they realise they rather like after all. The list of possible distractions is endless. And some founders may find they simply don't have what it takes. Maybe also the company needed cash at one point and one of the team had some spare and invested it.

All these factors need to be considered at the equity meeting. Here, the team must talk frankly about how much of the 'pie' they deserve and how much they think everyone else deserves.

Ideally, this meeting would be presided over by your mentor (much more on this essential person later in this chapter), who would have the final say in case of any disagreement.

This sounds like I'm being idealistic again, but actually many founding teams come to sensible decisions on this basis without acrimony, especially if they understand *from the start* that this is what is going to happen. People don't like to be offered a 33% stake in a company, then suddenly be told a few months later, out of the blue, that the rest of the team now considers that they are only worth 5%. But if they know from the start that the offer is provisional and that the stake will be discussed later, they are usually grown-up about the whole thing.

If they *don't* see sense . . . I'll talk about that in the next chapter.

Having established these stakes, *do all you can not to dilute them further*. Tony Waller, of global law firm CMS, observes: 'It's very easy, in the early days of a business, to treat equity like sweeties, and hand it out all over the place in return for very little value.' One of Tony's main jobs when taking on new clients (he works with high-tech start-ups) can be unscrambling the mess that has resulted from having doled out equity unthinkingly.

However, it can be very tempting to do this when you are short of cash. It often happens when the business suddenly needs something, and one of the cornerstones has a friend whom they reckon can provide it. I once did some work with a business that gave a 10% stake to someone who let them use their premises as an office. Usually these introductions turn out not to be as good as promised, and they soon disappear from view – with a chunk of your business in their pocket.

Tony advises that if you feel tempted to hand out equity this way, imagine yourself a few years down the line with a million pounds on the table. Will you really be happy giving away a hundred thousand pounds to this person?

In practice, most start-up shareholdings will end up with *some* dilution. When your part-time FD becomes full-time, they will need a decent-size stake. You may take on other cornerstones too, and proper cornerstones need a stake in the business. Once you start taking on more junior staff, they will need a (smaller) stake as well. More on stock options later. And you may have to trade equity for cash to finance expansion (though I am a huge fan of not doing this).

The Beermat sales funnel

After a while, you will probably work your way through the 'low-hanging fruit' of sales to personal contacts and have to start cold contacting. Some businesses are lucky enough not to have this problem. By the time they have sold to all their personal contacts, they have struck such a sweet spot that the network effect takes over. Word spreads around and they have potential customers, people they have never heard of, knocking on their door – thus proving that Kevin Costner's inner voice in *Field of Dreams* was right after all.

Most businesses don't experience this, however, and have to set up a formal sales system. Welcome to the Beermat sales funnel. This has ten levels, which may sound overcomplicated, but isn't. We don't do over-complicated in Beermat.

I use the image of the funnel because that is what it looks like: one of those things you use to put petrol in a small engine. It's wide at the top, narrowing down to a relatively small middle, then reasonably straight-edged for the last bit. People also talk about sales pipelines, but that's not a good metaphor, as one end of a pipeline is usually as large as the other. This is sadly not the case for sales, where you begin with a mouth-wateringly large list of prospects and end up with a few paying customers.

Once a business is doing well, it has prospects at each level in the funnel. Some have just handed the sales cornerstone a card at a networking meeting, while others are happy customers, just about to transfer the money to the enterprise's bank account. Everyone else is in between.

Level one

This is simply a list of prospects. By the time this book comes out, the laws on data storage and use (GDPR) will have radically changed, and at the time of writing there is uncertainty as to what will finally emerge as standard practice. So any advice given here has to be taken as provisional. It seems that the old sales technique of buying lists of prospect details will be either illegal, or, if the list is pre-screened in some way to make it compliant with the new regulations, will be costly. As an alternative, *if you are selling to business customers*, build your own list from directories, searching online, driving round local industrial estates – whatever it takes.

The new laws are particularly strict on gathering data about, and sending 'cold' emails to, private individuals, sole traders and partnerships.

It looks as if the 'magic email' route may be effectively closed for anyone selling to consumers or sole-trader businesses. Nothing is certain, however. The main target for GDPR is not small business but spammers and large organisations that 'farm' and sell personal data.

Level two

This is a *qualified* list, the level one list 'with brainwork applied'. The list will have been researched and broken down into relevant categories. Exactly what categories varies from situation to situation. Ideally, it's broken down by some sense of how likely they are to buy. Are they exactly in your target market? Are they local? Are they the size of business you imagined yourself serving?

Then learn about these individual prospects. Visit their websites.

The salesperson should call up and chat to whoever answers the phone in order to find out who is responsible for x (where x is the area with the pain that you are solving) and their email address. A magnet may well get a conversation going that yields more info about the business.

I used to advise that you keep thorough records of all you learn about prospects from this research. This is still an ideal to be striven for, and we shall have to wait and see exactly what the new rules allow in practice. My guess is that if you can demonstrate what the rules call a 'legitimate interest' in holding the information for a reasonable period of time, such record-keeping will be fine. But this is only a guess. Things should have become clearer by the time you have this book in your hands.

Everyone in the team should be networking. There should be a regular sales meet-up where everyone says if they have met any potential clients, or anyone from potential client organisations, and how they got on. If the answer is 'well', put these on the funnel at level two.

Go to trade shows as a simple attendee – you can take a small stand later, when you can afford it. You probably won't sell, but you can make contacts and learn. The people manning stands will vary, from the standoffish and rude to the bored-and-delighted-to-chat. Get the latter talking about their customers' needs. Maybe you could help them fulfil these needs.

Attend conferences. These need to be approached thoroughly. Go through the list of attendees beforehand and decide who you need to speak to. Task specific members of the team with connecting with specific individuals. When you make these connections, *don't sell*. Just connect. If you get on with someone, offer them something, such as a link to an interesting article or, ideally, an introduction to someone they would like to meet. In return, get their business card and ask permission to contact them.

Having built this qualified list, it's time to begin selling – gently.

The medium for this is the 'magic email', a personalised, individually crafted and legally compliant one. Not a ghastly piece of spam. I present a model of such an email at the back of the book. It says who you are, why you think the recipient would benefit from doing business with you (your mutual legitimate interest), offers them the chance to opt out of any further correspondence and suggests a short meeting.

Level three

This level of the funnel is when the email has been replied to positively and a meeting arranged.

Your level three meeting will be the same 15-minute, listening meeting that you had with your personal contacts. During it, the salesperson is discovering if the prospect has – or at least appears to have – the magic trio of needs and money today. They need to tick all three boxes. If they do, then they go up to level four.

Level four

At this level, the client says they have needs and money today.

But do they really? Does the person you're talking to actually have the power – or the real desire – to place an order?

If your planned sale is of something substantial, like a service contract, it may take a while working through the client's procurement system. This process will consume your time, energy, attention – and often money – and you cannot afford to waste these resources. You need to know as soon as possible if your smiling, eager-to-buy contact is actually going to turn out to be a time-waster, as well as an energy- and attention- and money-waster.

By far the easiest way to find this out is to try and make a small sale in the meantime. I call this the 'tiny thing'. A day of consultancy. A prototype. Some staff training on solving pain.

If the person you are speaking to won't buy this, then they have either been stringing you along for some reason (probably to do with internal politics), or they have much less authority than they led you to believe, or than your overoptimistic salesperson led themselves to believe. If someone is sufficiently senior in an organisation, they will have a budget to spend. That's how big organisations work, unless they are in financial crisis mode, in which case you don't want to be dealing with them anyway, unless you're in the financial rescue business. If they won't dip into this budget to try you out and see if you are actually any good, then something is wrong.

Level five

If they do place an order for the 'tiny thing', you are now at level five.

While you are delivering it, use the opportunity to start expanding your connection with the organisation. Get whoever runs your finance to have a chat with their FD or purchasing director, on the pretext of checking how their invoicing system works. Can your maker talk to some of their technical people?

Level six

The next level is reached when the tiny thing has been delivered, the customer is delighted and the money for the 'tiny thing' is in the bank.

Level seven

The seventh level is another meeting, probably the first of a series of meetings, to discuss the bigger sale you were after all along. Rather than an outsider pitching against a lot of other outsiders, you now have traction within the organisation. You delivered your tiny thing brilliantly. You made contacts while delivering. People will be getting to know and like you. They will want to do more business with you.

Level eight

This is when the client has agreed that you should deliver the bigger project.

It can happen that they end up ordering a scaled-down version of what you originally planned. This is fine, as you've still made a sale.

Note that if the project takes time, you should ask for step payments.

Level nine

This is when the project is delivered to the client's satisfaction.

Level ten

The last *tranche* of money is in the bank.

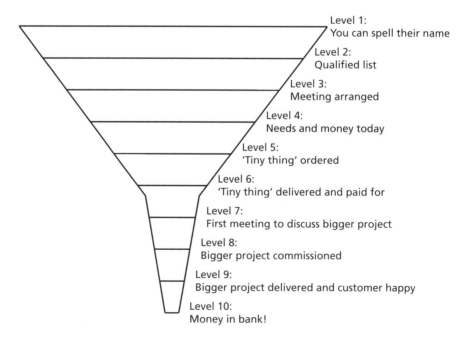

The Beermat sales funnel

Prospective sales will disappear from the funnel at all stages (though they shouldn't do so beyond level eight). Level two prospects don't agree to meetings. Meetings don't turn into sales. People won't buy tiny things. People buy tiny things, express delight but suddenly go quiet. A 'big project' meeting takes place but the client loses interest. Such is business.

There is a horrible alternative to this funnel. Some organisations, especially large ones, and double especially government ones, have complex and inflexible procurement procedures that they force everyone to squeeze through. You are fed into a ghastly sausage machine at the end of level four and have to pass an endless set of tests – pitches, beauty parades, shortlists and so on – which gobble up resources and have no guarantee of success at the end. I've known small businesses go bankrupt under the pressure of these. I call these the steps of misery. The 'tiny thing' sale at level five will help you get round these where possible or flag up 'steps of misery ahead' if you can't get round them.

If you must sell to such an organisation, make sure you have other, less exhausting sales on the go. Have someone very patient in charge of the process. If you are going to do 'steps of misery' sales a lot, find someone experienced in crafting and steering long, painful bids, and make them a critical factor cornerstone.

Consumer product sales

Much of the above section, with its talk of big orders, may seem biased towards selling to businesses. Maybe it is, but businesses selling products to consumers can face similar challenges.

Unless your sale is purely online, you will need to be in the shops. And that means selling to them, which in turn means meeting and building relationships with retail buyers. The supermarkets have a reputation for being ruthless, but they know that they need new products to keep their customers interested. Emma Killilea made her first sale to Sainsburys via its 'supply something new' initiative. She made her first contact with the company at a trade show where she had taken a small stand. One of their food product technologists tried a piece of gluten-free cake and liked it.

There are consultants who specialise in helping companies get a foot in 'big retail'. Check them out, but remember that in the end the relationship must be between you and the supermarket.

There are other routes to market. Supposing you have a wonderful mineral spring in your back garden which you want to bottle and sell. You could talk to local offices to see if they want water supplied to them. How about local caterers? You may need to think of clever ways of adding value to your product, providing the office with a dispenser which you undertake to fill regularly, or agreeing to provide the caterer with special bottles with 'Ethel and Fred, Silver Wedding' on. Be imaginative.

All these sales, from the biggest supermarket chain to the smallest local caterer, ultimately hinge on someone in an organisation liking your product and liking you. In other words, they rely on a salesperson. You can certainly help the salesperson by using a consultant to help you through the door, by creating a buzz about the product using social media, and by making sure it's attractively packaged. But in the end, it's about having a great product and then selling it, person to person, with persistence and charm.

What about being the retailer yourself? Arguably, a retailer needs to be a salesperson every moment, with each person who walks into their shop. But wider sales skills are often essential, too. A few large contracts can make the difference between failure and success. A friend of Chris's who ran a bookshop made his money supplying local schools, not from walk-in custom.

If you plan only to sell online, then maybe you can dispense with ever speaking to anyone. But some kind of customer service will usually be needed at some time – and you may find this is a way forward. Remember the Beermat maxim: 'Add service'. By selling a service as well as things, you get the chance to differentiate yourself from your rivals. But once you start adding service, you need someone to meet other people and convince them of the benefits of that service.

Your mentor

Your sales are beginning to build. You are now developing a clearer sense of what pain you are really solving, who for, and how you are actually doing it. This is the best time to find a mentor for the company. You are looking for someone with huge experience of business, who gets the point of what you're doing, who likes you and whom you like. They will provide you with lots of help and will do so for the love of it: if someone offers mentoring for a fee, then that's not mentoring but consultancy.

A mentor may even offer to invest, but don't expect this.

Later on, it will be wise to offer your mentor fees or an equity stake in the company in return for performing a formal role such as chair or non-executive director. But not yet.

I expect you are already imagining objections. I did when I first heard people talking about mentoring, but in retrospect my objections were all wrong. Here are some of them.

'Impossible – we don't know anyone like that'

Some entrepreneurs are lucky enough to come from entrepreneurial families. This is a real head start as you've grown up talking business over the dinner table. People in this situation often get wonderful mentoring from within their families. Failing that, they get lessons in how not to do it.

However, one of the aims of this book is to map out a path to success for *anybody* eager to get involved in entrepreneurship, whatever their current status or background. So maybe you're sitting here now and none of you knows anyone who falls into the category of potential mentor.

Relax. Finding a mentor is not impossible, it is simply a matter of will. If you make it a priority, and I'm saying that you must make it a priority, then you can find a mentor. In the process, you will learn a lesson that will prove of use again and again in all phases of business: the importance of making and pursuing priorities.

If you work in a particular industry you should have some idea of who among its successes is keen to help other businesses. If not, get such an idea fast. Maybe you have met one or some of these people in the course of your work. So approach them.

If there is nobody in your sector, try adjacent business sectors. The qualities for mentorship do not include 'works in your sector'. At the highest level, skill, thinking and contacts range across all types of business.

If you are starting from a very low base in terms of your current work – unemployed or very junior – it is harder to find a mentor of requisite quality. But not impossible. Set about your search slowly, systematically, imaginatively. All communities have leaders of various kinds. Who runs the chamber of commerce in your town? Your local religious leader may have a wealth of contacts you didn't know about. The Prince's Trust has an excellent mentoring system (see the section at the back of this book). Ask yourself who, among the people you can talk to, do you respect the most.

Students have no excuse for not finding a mentor. Your tutor should know people. Or get an interview with your vice-chancellor, who, if they care about their post (and most of them do) will be delighted to help enterprise within their college or university.

First-step contacts (local religious leader, college tutor) will not be mentors themselves, but they will know people who might be, or who in turn know people who might be. If you approach these people with seriousness and enthusiasm, they will move you towards the right person.

If you are *still* stuck for ideas, think of who has written a business book that inspired you, or think of a business you really admire and find out who the directors are. Then contact them. Avoid the obvious names. Sir Richard Branson probably gets hundreds of ideas fired at him every day.

'I don't want to deal with a load of old farts'

Someone in the founding team may say that. Someone who's fun but a bit immature probably. It's time they grew up and started taking people of all ages for what they are. The adventure of business success challenges everybody's preconceptions – class, gender, sexual orientation, age, race. That's one of the benefits of pursuing it.

Some excellent mentors are young, anyway. Since *The Beermat Entrepreneur* first came out, more and more young entrepreneurs have built great businesses, sold them and started mentoring.

But don't be ageist. Go for the best mentor you can, of any age.

'Supposing they nick the idea?'

This is an understandable fear when approaching people you don't know, but it is grossly overrated. When I worked at a launch network, almost all the entrepreneurs I met wanted me to sign a non-disclosure agreement before they would let me read their business plan. I used to explain that success is about having a good idea *and putting it into practice.* It was company policy not to sign such agreements anyway, as our reputation was based on integrity.

Once your idea is up and running and making money, *then* people will try to copy it. But don't worry about that now. I will talk about how to deal with those real copycats later.

Good mentors know this. They are also people who enjoy the business of putting ideas into practice. If they like your idea, they will be excited by the prospect of helping you make it work, not by the prospect of pinching it.

'I don't know what to say to someone like that'

Be yourself. Remember, you have a common passion with this person – business. If they are savvy – and most successful people are – they will pick this up and enjoy your enthusiasm.

Don't expect your target to pick up the phone when you call. Successful people surround themselves with 'firewalls', people trained to filter out time-wasters. Your first job is to persuade this firewall that you are not a time-waster. This is not as hard as it may sound, as you are not. And remember that the firewall is not just there to get rid of wasters but to facilitate welcome callers.

Begin by finding out who your potential mentor's PA is. Then send the PA a simple email explaining who you are, that you want five minutes of *their* (not their boss') time and ask them to suggest a time that would be convenient for you to call. If you get no reply, call them and leave a voicemail to this effect.

When you do speak to the PA, say that you want to speak to their boss because you believe you have a business idea that they would find interesting. Tell the PA your elevator pitch. Explain why you chose their boss (recommendation of vice-chancellor, loved his book, really admired the way she's restructured Megacorp's food division). Don't lie. It'll show and you will look ridiculous. If you are sincere that will shine through too.

A good PA will either set up a brief conversation or say no and explain why. It may be that you have not expressed yourself clearly enough, which gives you the opportunity to restate your pitch. Or maybe their boss is not interested in mentoring, in which case thank the PA politely. You can ask if they know of anyone in their organisation who would be interested.

If the PA is rude, then that's a clear sign that their boss was not for you anyway. The kind of people who make good mentors employ polite, intelligent PAs, not human Rottweilers.

'Can't we just skip this and get on with it?'

No. A mentor is worth their weight in gold. They can be the difference between an idea's success and failure.

Remember that the qualities you will use and develop in the search for your mentor – confidence, persistence, single-mindedness, sincerity – will be of enormous use in business later on.

So let the doubters have their say, then get on with finding a mentor. No excuses.

The qualities of a mentor

Experience

I discovered the true value of mentoring when working for a software company. Soon after joining, I turned up at work one morning to find a white-haired gentleman sitting in the chairman's office. I actually wondered if this was somebody's dad who'd come up to London for the day and was just sitting in an empty office, waiting to join them for lunch. Then I was told this was Sir Campbell Fraser, former Chairman of Dunlop, Tandem and Scottish Television, and President of the CBI. His role? Mentor to the company.

Sir Campbell later became a personal mentor to me. He was the best source of business advice I ever met, having seen all kinds of business in all kinds of areas, and understanding the basic unchanging principles both of commerce and of human nature. Sadly, he died back in 2007. I still miss him, and his kindly, generously shared wisdom, hugely.

They get your idea

The mentor must get your idea. In a perfect world, they would react to it with the same excitement as the entrepreneur's mates did in the pub. But they're more experienced and wiser, so they will be much more considered. If they like you and the idea, they'll go away and assess the assumptions and logic behind it.

If they don't get the idea, move on and try someone else. Never fob yourself off with someone impressive-sounding person who *quite likes* the idea. As every salesperson knows, 'maybe' is the worst possible answer. A clear no sets you free to look elsewhere, while an enthusiastic yes means you're in business. Close the deal properly with your mentor: you are going to ask a lot of them, and they will only deliver if their belief is real.

They must like you

How do you know if they like you? You just have to use your intuition here. You have a lot to offer them in terms of energy and liveliness, so offer it and watch them respond. Remember that they won't see you as rivals as they've been there and done it anyway. People like kindred spirits. Share your enthusiasm.

You must like them

As above, trust your intuition. Whoever wrote 'I do not love you, Dr Fell, But how or why, I cannot tell' gave the doctor a wide berth, if they had any sense. Don't allow anyone or anything to override your intuition. 'They're very respected' or 'Lots of other people speak highly of them.' So what?

Intuition doesn't get a lot of space in business literature, maybe because it's impossible to draw complicated diagrams of it, complete with triangles, cut-away cylinders, more arrows than Custer's last stand and the word 'synergy' somewhere. But it's hugely valuable, especially in dealing with people. Its lack of definability makes it hard to measure, or to improve once you have made an assessment of it.

This might appear bad news, but my experience of intuition is that almost everybody has it to a very high degree, and that the people who make bad judgements are the ones who override it in some way. I've so often heard people say something like 'There was something about them I didn't like, but logically they seemed just right, so I went along with them. It all went wrong, of course.' If you make a run of bad judgements, ask yourself what you are putting in the way of your natural talent for spotting fakes and phonies.

Note that business has already ceased to be about spreadsheets and software, and has entered the world of personal judgement and emotions. Is this world 'simple'? As I said above, you have intuition. Trust it.

Mentor qualities

- Experienced and senior business person
- Gives, not sells, their time
- Gets your idea
- Likes you – shares your enthusiasm
- You like them

What a mentor offers

At the most basic, a mentor offers *good advice*. They will have seen similar ideas before and will have an understanding about practical difficulties, and most important, how to get round these difficulties. They will have a broad view of the business marketplace and will understand where your idea fits in.

They may know someone who is likely to be an early customer – not just a company but an individual person within that company. This is where the mentor really earns your undying gratitude: *connections*. Your mentor will send you direct to someone with serious influence and they will do so *with a personal endorsement*. When you go to meet this person, the whole founding team should come along.

Your mentor's connections are also essential if you need to raise *capital*. The mentor may invest themselves – this is particularly common where the mentor is a successful entrepreneur – or suggest to personal, wealthy friends that they do so. Later, if necessary, they can put you in touch with business angels.

Mentors are also invaluable in helping you find sources of *specialist advice* (more on this later in this chapter).

Finally, having a highly respected figure on your side gives your business extra *credibility*.

In finding such a person you have leapt another hurdle on your way to success.

What mentors bring

- Advice
- Connections to
  - customers
  - sources of finance
  - outside experts
- Credibility

Why do people become mentors? Because they enjoy it. Obviously, it's not every successful business person's flute of Bollinger, and you will spot non-mentors very quickly, as they really do not want to be bothered by people they consider wannabes. But it suits many people perfectly. As a mentor, you can take part in a new business venture, without having the total, exhausting and risky involvement that the founding team has.

Mentors have a strong desire to pass on the lessons they have learnt, especially to people in whom they see at least partial reflections of themselves.

Make sure that your mentor gets what they want out of mentoring. You can do this by doing the following:

- **Make it easy for them**: Meet at a time and a place that suits them, not you.
- **Take their advice**: Sadly I have mentored some people who have not done this, or worse, who have started playing the 'Yes, but . . . ' game, where they throw advice back in my face, adding that I haven't understood how difficult life is for them or quite how brilliant they are.
- **Say thank you**: I've had mentees who didn't even bother to thank me. (If this is beginning to turn into a whinge-fest on my part, most of the people I mentor are great.)

Finding a mentor is not always easy, but it is worth every moment you put into the search, many times over.

Some lucky people can have the opposite problem in that they have too many people wanting to mentor them. I used to think that you had to whittle this down to one person and keep it that way, but on reflection why deprive yourself of help (and deprive nice people of the pleasure of helping you)?

I do think that the seedling business is best with one principal mentor. You show commitment to them by taking their advice first, and as the business grows they are the first person to be asked to become chair. But as the business grows it also gets more complex, and you will have a range of issues, some of which are in areas where your principal mentor will not be an expert. They may well send you to someone else for help with that issue. Or go out and find someone.

Over the years I have gathered around me a small group of people whose advice and expertise I trust deeply. I believe I have done the same for others and become part of their mentoring circle.

An early joiner of your mentoring circle will be that most valuable of advisers, your *customer mentor.* Customer mentors will also tell you honestly if you are doing something wrong (other customers may not tell you this, and instead simply stop buying). They will suggest improvements such as new features or new services you could add. They will offer endorsements and, even more valuable, referrals. If you are selling to large organisations they may act as your ambassador within that organisation, figuratively (and sometimes even literally) showing you around, suggesting who to talk to on specific issues – and who to avoid and how.

Many customers want to do this, but sales cornerstones often miss out on the opportunity. Sometimes this is because the salespeople think such offers are too good to be true. They aren't. The customer mentor gets pay-offs too. If they bring a good product into the organisation, they will be respected for that. If you provide a good pain-solving product, you help them do their job. And if you're nice, they'll enjoy your company. Wins all round.

Accept them and enjoy building the relationship.

When you write the name of your mentor on your original beermat, underneath the elevator pitch and the name of your first customer, you have written your first business plan.

The Beermat ethos

You are now getting seriously stuck in to business, so I should say a bit about how to compete. Competition is good. It drives innovation and stops organisations becoming smug, self-serving and arrogant towards their customers. But there comes a point where competitiveness becomes destructive, both to the business and to the individuals practising it.

I believe there are four cardinal principles that you should adhere to. If you find yourself being coerced into denying these principles, or just drifting into so doing, then you know it is time to take stock and change. Get out of any situation that has put you in this position.

The first is the old *golden rule.* Treat others as you would like to be treated. This rule is enjoined on believers by almost every religion in the world, as well as being recommended by humanist philosophers.

The second is *tell the truth*. The temptation in business to be dishonest can be strong but it needs to be resisted. This is a practical as well as a moral rule. Business is based on trust, which is something that can take a long time to build but a short time to destroy once someone starts lying (or is exposed to have been lying). In my earlier career selling, I didn't always tell the truth, and nearly always paid a price for it later. People aren't stupid – they find things out.

A third maxim is *help people when you can*. This is rather less absolute than the above two, as an element of judgement is required. There is so much need in the world that we could spend all our time, money and effort in helping others and getting nothing back other than a nice feeling. However, if you can do so without detriment to yourself and to your connections, then give it.

Start-ups need all the help they can get, and my sense is that the more you help others, the more people are likely to help you. Word gets around. While working in corporate-land, Martin Dawson was generous with advice for people needing to know more about marketing. When he launched Broker's Gin, he felt at ease asking others for help, and found many people willing to provide it.

The fourth is *don't do negative talk*. When you start selling your product, you will inevitably hear people say that your stuff is a bit like the models that ABC make. Imagine these two responses:

- **Salesperson A**: Them! We hate those guys. Their stuff is rubbish.
- **Salesperson B**: Oh, yes, ABC. I've heard they're a good company and make a decent product. But our product offers these special benefits . . .

It sounds obvious which is the more mature approach, but I have heard and been horrified by adult, highly paid salespeople reacting like A.

Customers may well know people in ABC and will probably have been using their products quite happily for years. Are you telling them they're stupid? Worse, this might be a trap, by someone wanting you to say something negative about ABC which they can then use as ammunition in some game with you or someone else. Customers are not interested in squabbles between suppliers but they are interested in getting their needs met. If you can do better than your rivals, prove it in a positive way.

The Beermat way is that business competition should be at a level where you can have a drink with the opposition and conduct a proper conversation with them. Sport played in the right spirit has the same credo. Hard, fair competition on the field and a drink in the bar afterwards. My own sporting hero Jason Leonard was noted for this.

Doing business the Beermat way

- Treat others as you would like to be treated
- Tell the truth
- Help other people where sensibly possible
- Avoid negative talk
- Hard but fair

Some people may scoff at these maxims and quote WC Fields, 'Never give a sucker an even break', adding perhaps that 'Food needs to be put on the table'. The latter comment is certainly true, but this book is about how to put food – and lots of nice food – on the table in an ethical way. There are people who are proud of being the biggest bully on the block and who do make money. I can't pretend this doesn't happen. But it's not the Beermat way. I suspect such people don't have very happy lives. They seem to go through an awful lot of partners and their children aren't always very fond of them.

Supposing you find yourself up against someone who rips up the rule book? There are some damaged people out there. You have to be prepared to fight for your business. If you are an entrepreneur, I don't need to tell you this. It's deep in your bones, anyway. In this fight, you may find yourself slipping down the dark side, twisting the truth, obsessing about an opponent. Try and rise above this. However, at the same time, dark energy can be used in a positive way. Let it spur you to extra action, not vengefulness. Stay focused on your customers. One point of dirty tricks is to take your eye off the ball, which is serving your customers ever better.

If someone starts spreading malicious rumours about you, that is an opportunity to reconnect with your customers and tell them that the rumours are totally false. They will appreciate the fact that you have done so.

I cover two other classic nasties – price wars and theft of intellectual property – elsewhere in this book (in Chapter 3: The sapling enterprise, and later in this chapter).

Actual intimidation or physical attacks on staff should of course be reported at once to the police. If they use other kinds of underhand tactics, remember that people who do this usually get found out and their loss of credibility can be massive.

In the past decade, a number of entrepreneurs have been on the end of shameful treatment by banks (tales are now beginning to emerge of quite how shameful). I'm happy to believe that most bank employees want to do a decent, fair job, but there seem to have been some seriously rotten apples in the industry. Maybe these have now all been cleared out. But suspicion remains – such is the long-lasting effect of past malpractice. The best protection against abuse of power by financial institutions is to have a really able finance cornerstone (more on this below) and to listen to what they say.

Seedling finance

The founding team should become financially literate and understand certain basic principles of the money side of things. You're starting a business, for heaven's sake! Read our guide, *Finance on a Beermat*.

And here are some tips from our finance manager at The Instruction Set, Rick Medlock:

- Always borrow on long term if you can. An overdraft can be called in at any time whereas a lease or a three-year term loan gives you certainty of cashflow.
- Do a monthly cashflow forecast and always take a gloomier picture than your worst estimates.
- Try to persuade suppliers to give you extra payment terms – 60 rather than 30 days to pay.
- Don't mess with the VAT people, HMRC or the DWP. If you get on the wrong side of them, they will be after you for ever and will scrutinise everything you do or claim.
- Get your systems and documentation processes right from day one. Too many people simply start, then worry about the audit trail or evidence for expenses afterwards. This inevitably leads to problems. Set up simple systems on day one. These can be upgraded as you grow.
- Don't spend money that you don't have in the vain hope that money will be found somewhere. *This is the quickest route to bankruptcy.* If you haven't actually got the cash today, don't spend it.
- Treat capital expenditure even more suspiciously than day-to-day expenses. Ignore the fact that these assets last for more than one year (and therefore you think they are worth something to someone else). The truth is that used kit, especially computers, is basically worth zilch to anyone else. Remember that the cash goes out of the door on day one. Try to lease stuff by all means but remember you have to keep paying that lease for as long as the lease lasts.
- Whether you are borrowing or not, keep the bank well-informed and up to date on progress, and again give them good information so that if you want to borrow to expand they know you and your business and they trust you.

Sir Campbell's financial advice to start-ups was even more succinct: 'Watch the cash, laddie.'

As I've said, get a part-time bookkeeper quickly. As you begin to grow, hire a part-time financial director. This person needs to spend a day a month with the team. They should do a rough cashflow forecast, advise on the tax and legal implications of any plans, and be consulted on any expenditure. They will help in any dealings with the bank.

You need to like your part-time FD and for them to like you. As the business grows further, they will spend more time with you. They become your finance cornerstone. If the business grows as far and as fast as you hope, they are the person to whom you will first offer the job of full-time FD.

Right now, your part-time FD will want to be paid for their work, but you can try offering a package of some cash plus a promise that if the business really takes off, the full-time job will be theirs, with an appropriate salary, responsibility and an equity stake.

Seedling funding

At The Instruction Set we built a 150-person company without *any* outside funding, apart from a bank loan to get us going.

I recommend you move heaven and earth to do the same, partly because external funding is a nightmare, but also because refusing to rely on it imposes a discipline on the business that is very, very healthy. Do you really need that smart new piece of kit? Will a second-hand one not be just as good? Check out the prices on eBay. Or don't buy at all and just hire. That way, if things go wrong, which they still might for a fragile young seedling, you can return them and have no debts outstanding. Better still, can you borrow it, bartering it for some other current or future favour? Entrepreneur Steve Sampson says 'At this time in the business' life, your motto has to be *Make do and mend.*'

Some entrepreneurs can become fixated on the appearance of the brand and want to spend money on this straightaway. Customers, by and large, aren't too worried as they just want their pain solved. Even in consumer markets, if a product is excellent and original, a good enough design will get things moving. (Big expensive designers don't always get it right, either.) Broker's Gin started off being sold in a bottle designed by founder Martin Dawson. Oppo Ice Cream started the opposite way, using a big-name designer but finding the result didn't work in stores, and ending up working with a local designer. Save substantial expenditure on this till you're making decent money and doing so consistently.

Having put in some cash to comprise the original share capital and to get the whole business going, the founding team now need to put in sweat equity, working unpaid to begin with, driving around in their own vehicles rather than leasing 'company' ones (check this is OK with your insurer) and working from home rather than a rented office.

By contrast, I have seen aspiring entrepreneurs pitch for funding, and when asked what the money would go on, reply that it, or a serious chunk of it, would go to pay them while they got things going. I have not seen any potential funders impressed by this.

I know that software and other technology companies will find it hard to follow the 'fund from revenue' route, as they need substantial upfront capital. But, as I have said, if they take a Beermat approach, they will look at all possible ways of funding from revenue before getting substantial external funding. Can they, for example, set up some kind of services arm to fund the development of the core project?

This was essentially our plan at The Instruction Set, and we ended up concentrating on the services. I've even met a biotech company following this model. There are two businesses, one of which provides assistance with drug trials and yields cash, while the other spends the cash developing products.

Here is my Beermat list of seedling funding sources. It is in descending order of desirability rather than of how things will most likely happen. In a perfect world, you would have very little bank lending, but in reality, you will probably need it at times.

Revenue

First, by far the best, is revenue. If you have an offer that sounds capable of solving real pain, ask for payment in advance. Your customer may need reassurance on quality and delivery. Provide it. You want to be the best anyway. They may ask for a discount for this kind of payment. As long as the discount isn't ridiculous, agree.

We secured a healthy chunk of early finance this way at The Instruction Set, selling our first Advanced UNIX course to a client in Sweden. We hadn't actually written the course at the time, and soon after receiving the advance payment, one of our gurus fell ill. We had to get the course ready by hook or by crook. And we did. I remember the day before the course was due to begin, sitting in our office punching holes in pages and putting them into loose-leaf binders. The plane was due to leave in two hours. But of course that's exactly the adventure of starting a business.

Competitions, grants and government loans

Second is competitions, grants or government loans.

Emma Killilea won a number of competitions, including the UK National Student Entrepreneur Award, which covered the start-up costs of Delicious Alchemy.

At the time of writing, small businesses are able to apply for government loans via www.startuploans.co.uk. You can apply for up to £25,000, and successful applicants also get mentoring for 12 months.

If you are unemployed, ask about the Enterprise Allowance Scheme.

Check out The Prince's Trust. It is an excellent organisation, which really does want to help young people with bright ideas. See the section on it at the back of this book.

Ask around. There may be local schemes in your part of the country.

Your money

Third is your own money. Yes, you will need to put a small amount in to get things moving. After that, in a perfect world, you would fund all but the very first business expenses from revenue or the right kind of hand-out. Further commitment of your own money would be not directly to the business, but indirectly, using it to keep yourself afloat while the business begins to grow but is still too cash-strapped to pay you for your work. However, more personal investment may well be needed. Be prepared for this.

Family

Fourth is family. I put this below your own cash because to do so is better discipline. If you've had to work hard for the cash you're putting in, you will be more ruthless in taking tough financial decisions at the margin that can make the difference between success and failure. However, family money is still very welcome. A lot of businesses start with a bit of support from this source.

Friends

Fifth is friends. Families (who are stuck with you, as you are with them) can be more forgiving than friends if the money disappears. But it won't, will it?

Your mentor

Sixth is your mentor. If your mentor really likes you and your idea, they might make an investment themselves. They are part of the team, and this investment cements the relationship. However, it is essential that you do not initially approach your mentor with this in mind. What you want from them is mentoring. If, having established a good working relationship with you, they offer some cash, that is a delightful added extra.

Friends of your mentor

Your mentor may also have friends who are interested in investing.

Bank lending

Next is bank lending. Most seedling businesses get some money from the bank. We did at The Instruction Set. If they are wise, they pay this off as soon as possible.

When looking for a bank, shop around. Banking was once effectively a cartel but has recently been shaken up by ambitious outsiders like Metro Bank. What you are looking for is not the best rates (they still won't be that different), but a person whom you like, who likes you and who gets your idea. Talk to other small business owners and ask who they bank with and why.

In an ideal world, you borrow from the bank to finance expansion of some kind, not to cover start-up costs. Banks like to see an account with some money coming into it, and then lend.

There are basically two types of bank lending. One is an overdraft, the other is a formal loan.

Overdrafts are there to iron out any bumps in income flow or to help with a sudden, short-term need for some extra working capital or for an essential but small item. They are *not* there to be blown at once – though I've seen businesses do that. If you are always near your overdraft limit, you are not getting the real benefit from it, which is financial flexibility. The ideal overdraft is only used sporadically as the account dips in and out of credit.

A sensible level of overdraft to ask for is the amount of cash you usually spend in a month.

The downside of overdrafts is two-fold. They can be called in at any time, without much explanation. Banks will argue that they only do this to companies that are about to fail, but it's not a nice threat to have hanging over your head. Also, overdrafts carry a higher rate of interest than the second source of bank funding, loans.

Loans are for longer-term financial needs. They should be for specific reasons, for example, to buy a machine or to fund an expansion into a new market. Their structure should reflect this. If you are planning to use the machine for three years, the loan should be repayable over that period.

In the long run, banks prefer loans to overdrafts. Loans are usually secured on an asset, and loan repayments also include some capital. So if a borrower goes broke half way through the loan, the bank will have got some of its money already and can take the asset. Warning! If you have been running a large overdraft for a while, the bank may try to convert at least some of it into a loan. This is not good news if you are planning to expand and actually need a bigger overdraft to cover this.

There is often a culture clash between banks and entrepreneurs. Bank managers like spreadsheets, regular income flows and predictability, while entrepreneurs like brainstorming sessions (led by them), big deals and the thrill of the unexpected. The solution is to sit the most process-minded member of the team down with *Finance on a Beermat* and then get them to deal with the bank. When you can afford it, get a part-time finance director and have them handle this relationship.

Do all you can to avoid banks taking charges on your property when you start, and on your firm's assets as you grow (except for the case above where a loan is specifically taken out to fund an asset). We had to go down this route at The Instruction Set and had a party when we got a letter from the bank – after much pressing – saying they no longer sought a charge on our personal assets but would take one against the company's assets instead.

In good times, banks may try and interest you in new financial products or just offer to lend you more money than you need. Be wary of this, as if times change, they can suddenly get nasty.

Crowdfunding

Last on this list is crowdfunding. This is a popular new way of getting money for a business though it has a long history. The Statue of Liberty was partially crowdfunded. I've only put it low on the list because it works better for some types of business than for others.

It works well for companies making things for consumers, especially high-end, top-quality things. Oppo Ice Cream has had three funding rounds using the Seedrs crowdfunding site.

The process needs to be managed. Oppo co-founder Harry Thuillier comments: 'You can't just put up a page and hope. You have to talk to people beforehand and get them excited.' Do this. Get a spreadsheet, listing everyone who has said they'd invest and how much they promised. Tell them when the crowdfunding page is due to go up and remind them of their promise when it does. Have a good video on the page to rekindle the excitement that people felt when you were pitching to them. One of Oppo's rounds hit its target in two minutes thanks to this approach – a record which itself earned the company good media coverage.

Oppo investors are also evangelists, committed to telling the world about the ice cream and how wonderful it is.

High-profile artists with fans can also use this route. Rock band Marillion were among the first modern users of crowdfunding to finance a US tour. Unbound is a successful UK-based publisher which uses the model, crowdfunding each book. Social enterprises can also crowdfund successfully.

For technology companies there is a fear that crowdfunding makes it necessary to release too much information, too widely, too soon, increasing the risk of IP theft. There are also difficulties attached to having lots of small shareholders.

If you are a service company, my advice is to stick to the basics and *fund from revenue*.

Bigger beasts

What about those bigger beasts of the funding world, business angels and venture capitalists? I shall cover these in Chapter 3: The sapling enterprise. Most seedling businesses do not need to have dealings with these people.

Technology start-ups may have to enter this lion's den earlier – as a rule of thumb if they want more than £100,000 of funding. They should tread carefully. Some angels are truly angelic, but others aren't.

The Beermat guide to seedling finance

1. Revenue
2. Grants or 'soft' loans
3. Your own money
4. Family
5. Friend(s)
6. Mentor
7. Friend of mentor
8. Bank loan to get things started (pay off asap).
9. Subsequent bank funding. Overdraft for extra working capital and loans for specific items or projects
10. Crowdfunding

The law

Use your solicitor for essential legal work such as partnership agreements, leases and warranties. The best lawyers have standard formulae for these: boilerplate contracts with schedules to particularise them. These should cost hundreds rather than thousands of pounds. Bad lawyers string work out so don't let them get away with this.

Lawyers who do string work out sometimes complain that they have been given such a poor brief that it's taken them all this time to understand what their clients really want. Maybe that's true, so don't leave yourself open to this response. Be crystal clear with these guys.

As with banks, once you have chosen, get the finance cornerstone or their nearest equivalent, the most process-minded of the team, to deal with them.

Patents

If you have a good idea, people will try to steal it. That's a fact of life. At The Instruction Set we came across a company that had copied our training manuals word for word, even down to our own names in the examples. We hired a detective from Pinkerton's to go in and check the story, then threatened to sue them for breach of copyright.

The problem is that most theft of intellectual property (IP) is rather subtler than this. Once a piece of plagiarism amends an original work by quite a small amount, it ceases legally to be theft.

For service businesses, the best protection of IP is execution. Not, sadly, of the copycats, but in your business: the speed and quality of your delivery. If you are genuinely the first person with an idea, you should be able to bring it to market quickest. That's your initial protection: being there first. But that's only the start, as enthusiasts of first mover advantage can find out.

Once you are there, make sure you deliver superbly – on time and in an efficient, friendly, business-like manner. If you do this, a copycat who contacts your customers saying they do it too will probably be sent away, even if they are cheaper. People don't like changing suppliers, and only do so if the motive is strong. Such motives include continuing poor delivery, excessive prices, a step change in the market that renders the product obsolete – or, strange but true, being ignored. Poor farming, ignoring customers, is a surprisingly common cause of loss of business.

Inevitably, there will come a time when there are me-too products around. Don't be dragged into a price war (more on this in Chapter 3: The sapling enterprise) or endless litigation. Keep improving the product and its delivery and keep in touch with your customers. At the same time, take obvious precautions against IPR theft by writing © on documents like course materials and by registering trademarks.

In the software and other technology-driven sectors, the need for patenting is much more pressing. Your intellectual property may represent the essence of your business. Get a good patent lawyer who understands your technology at least as well as you do, and work with them to create a portfolio of patents. This could become hugely valuable if you sell the business.

Tony Waller observes that drafting a strong patent requires a highly specialist skill-set, not just in the sense of specialising in patent law but deeper, in the sense of specialising in patent work *within specific sectors* like software and biotech. Take time to research who are the best patent lawyers in your sector.

Pure ideas cannot be patented. Entrepreneurs often think they have totally original ideas and are terrified that someone will steal them. Actually, very few ideas are totally original. And if they are, they may not be good *business* ideas as they might be too far ahead of the market. Leonardo da Vinci didn't get rich out of flying machines. But even if the idea is original and relevant, it is only the beginning of the journey to commercial success. Remember Edison's remark about genius being 1% inspiration and 99% perspiration.

By contrast, you can lose out by being too reticent about an idea. Let the word get around that you are on to something (though nobody's quite sure what), and able people will check you out. Some may want to help you in some way or become part of the team. Customer interest might be aroused. If you have a patent lawyer, they will be able to give guidance on how to attract the right attention to your business without running the risk of harming your ability to patent your technology.

Litigation

Don't litigate, negotiate.

The sad truth about litigation is that once you end up in a court, you have already lost. Only the lawyers win. And the media if there's a celebrity involved. If you are on the verge of litigation, stop and ask why. Then sort the problem another way.

Legal problems often arise from poor communication. When you made that deal which is now being so furiously argued over, both parties intended to benefit from it. You would get money and your customer would get a product that was of use to them. So what has gone wrong? It's time to start negotiating.

Initial deals – and many subsequent deals – are often not based on formal, legally binding contracts. The acceptance is usually verbal. This can lead to problems later unless you take sensible steps to put some kind of formal shape to the agreement.

The first thing to do is to draw up a memorandum of understanding (also known as a heads of agreement). This outlines what you intend to deliver, and how and when and to what standard, and what and how and when the customer intends to pay for it. However, it is not legally binding unless specifically written that way. This memorandum cements the relationship with the client. If clients refuse to agree to it, this is a real danger signal that they might be time-wasters, simply trying to gain free market information or up to some internal political game in their own organisation.

Once delivery begins, your sales cornerstone must monitor the process. Is the customer happy? Are things working out as planned? Keep a record of meetings and conversations, so if things do get nasty, you have a record of what occurred (though even these are of limited use in court). Remember the story of Theseus, who laid a trail of silk behind him when he went into the Minotaur's labyrinth. The Minotaur, a beast with a bull's head and a man's body which ate nothing but human flesh, was a lot less scary than most corporate lawyers.

The moment you begin to suspect things aren't going to plan, talk to the client. And listen to them. Some clients try it on but most don't. Maybe you're not delivering quite what they expected, or the product isn't working as well as expected, or their own needs are changing. Deal with these issues.

Note the importance of keeping the sales cornerstone involved with the customer. Large businesses selling direct to consumers hand these customers over from sales to customer services the moment the sale is made. This is annoying enough if you buy baked beans, and appalling practice in a small, business-to-business organisation. At Micromuse, a software company I did some work for, the sales team saw all the trouble tickets produced by customer services, even when the company went public and had a huge range of customers.

Many problems occur when customers suggest *changes to a product*. Make sure they know as soon as possible the cost implications of making these changes. Give them a genuine figure – don't estimate for the sake of speed, but ask the relevant technician. Sometimes apparently easy changes can be expensive.

Clients sometimes suggest these changes because they are really needed, but not always. The suggestion can be more of an enquiry. I have seen huge ill feeling caused by semi-serious enquiries being taken seriously. The customer says in an idle moment 'Supposing the widgets were green'. The supplier mistakes this for a formal request, repaints them all, then sends in a bill. The customer refuses to pay . . .

Of course, the customer is fully entitled to change their mind. They're paying. Don't resent these changes, as they are part of the process of making your offer exactly what they want. But always make sure the customer understands the cost implications of any suggestions.

If you do get stuck in one of these traps, negotiate your way out of it. Remember that in good negotiation, both sides win. Negotiators who flatten the opposition win – in the short term, but don't expect to do business with the losers again.

Other advisers

As the business grows, you should develop a small group of trusted external advisers. Your solicitor will be one. For a technology company, your patent lawyer will be another. When you start employing people, a good HR consultant is invaluable. Entrepreneurs wanting to sell to consumers will need a good designer.

Ask around. Who's good? Meet a few. Use your intuition. Who do you like? Who 'gets' you and what your business is trying to do?

Have them do a tiny thing first. If this works, do a deal with them. Don't nail them to the floor but remind them that you are a growing company and will be putting lots more business their way over time. Mean this.

Stay loyal to good advisers whom you like. Make them part of the family.

Advisers on a Beermat

- Ask around
- Choose someone you like and who 'gets' you
- Have them do a tiny thing
- Do a deal
- Stay loyal

For any advisers reading this, note that working with entrepreneurs can be fun but will be challenging. Be very hands-on. Let the entrepreneur enjoy working with you. But keep some distance. Remember that you are the expert.

Marketing

Most entrepreneurs want to spend money on marketing and turn their beloved business into a brand. That's fine as long as you do it at the right time, which is once you know exactly who you are and what the brand is really about. And also once you have a revenue stream that a) means you can afford marketing costs, and b) shows that people out there like your offer enough to pay for it. I've seen lots of money wasted on premature marketing.

If you are selling goods to consumers, this moment will come sooner than if you are selling services to business. But even FMCG (fast-moving consumer goods) entrepreneurs spend a long time getting the product spot on before spending lots of money on branding.

Of course, all businesses need some marketing basics quickly. An elegant, informative, user-friendly website. Decent business cards. As long as you can get one designed cheaply, a company logo. Notepaper for formal communication.

A decent website is easy to build yourself if one of the team likes the idea of so doing, or to have built if nobody does. If you hire a web designer, follow the rules above for advisers.

Many seedling websites are essentially brochures, which you tell people to visit once they have met you. Getting people you don't know to visit the site can be tricky. The rules of SEO (search engine optimisation) are always changing in an arms race between Google and SEO practitioners, which means that SEO work can be expensive and can date quickly. Unless you are a pure internet business, do some simple Beermat SEO yourself. Here's how:

- **Keywords**: Google provides free tools to help you choose keywords. Use these in your blogs and text, but don't let them spoil the flow and quality of the writing. Google is becoming ever better at distinguishing between properly written content that uses keywords intelligently and rubbish stuffed with them.
- **Links**: Link to other respected, relevant sites.
- **Keep active**: Google loves activity – site visits, new blogs. Blogs can be quite short (Google currently likes about 300 words, though this may change). Keep the blogs fresh. If you find yourself saying the same thing over and over again, step back. Alongside the shorter blogs, have a few longer, deeper pieces about key issues in your sector. You want your site to be the go-to place for people who want expert, relevant, carefully thought-out material.

Obviously, make your site easy to navigate. I say 'obviously', but there are still loads of sites that don't do this, which is disrespectful to the visitor.

Someone in the founding team will no doubt be eager to leap into social media. This needs to be done thoughtfully and there is a section on this in Chapter 3: The sapling enterprise.

Two magic lists

I talked about your list of prospects in the section on the sales funnel. This is an incredibly valuable resource and needs to be kept fresh and full. However, over time, two other lists become essential to the business.

Newsletter list

The first is what I call your newsletter list. You should be gathering email addresses from people all the time, not just prospects but anyone who expresses an interest in the company, your products or anything related to you, really. These go on a list which you use to send out some kind of newsletter.

Don't make it dull. Do make it regular, though it doesn't have to appear that often – what matters is that it doesn't just dry up, and that when it does arrive, it's actually interesting. Do make it legal, making sure that recipients have opted in to receiving it (if you are in doubt about the rules for this, ask around or have a chat with your solicitor). Don't use it to sell aggressively. A useful rule is once you have provided three pieces of information that people will find genuinely useful or enjoy, you can allow yourself a bit of gentle selling. The main point of the newsletter is to remind readers that you are in business and that you are getting ever better at it.

Network list

The second, and most important list is that of your network. An individual's personal network should be around 150 people (I say more on this number in Chapter 4: The mighty oak), and so should that of the business. It will comprise the 150 people who most know, like and trust it. Your mentor and advisers of course. Favourite customers, especially customer mentors. Key suppliers. Technology experts you admire and who like you. Influencers and ambassadors.

These last two terms can be confused. *Influencers* are people – journalists, bloggers – who are widely listened to in the sector you intend to serve. Do your research: who are they, and which of them is likely to be sympathetic to you? It may be you want to knock some of them off their perch by shaking things up. But others will probably be sympathetic. Contact the latter and arrange a brief meeting. Get them on board.

Ambassadors are people who like to spread the word about you. They overlap with influencers, of course, but can be different. A customer who loves you and tells their friends and colleagues may not command the industry-wide attention of a well-known 'influencer', but will loyally bat for you as far as they can.

Influencers can be fickle. Ambassadors are more likely to stick around. Both matter, however.

Take time and effort to build and to curate your network list. It will become one of the most valuable things that your business possesses.

Don't just send out standard newsletters to your network. Personal contact should be made every two months. This can be by email, but not a standard one. Have a designated team member whose job it is to oversee this.

Other lists will include Facebook friends and Twitter and Instagram followers. These are useful resources, too, but not as important as the above lists, unless you are a totally web-based business.

The Beermat list of lists

- Prospects list
- Newsletter list
- The business' own network: 150 key individuals
- Lists on social media

The real business plan

The business has been going a while now. That seedling is looking very healthy, and well on its way to being a metre in height. It's time to formalise things a little more. What is the business about? Where does it sit in the commercial landscape? Who are its key people? Above all, where is it heading?

I've already expressed my dislike of 70-page business plans for products that have not yet made any sales. But once the business knows what it's about, then it is time to sit down and plan its future more thoughtfully, though never losing sight of the fact that the unexpected often happens. Enter what I call the 'real business plan' to distinguish it from the many fantasy business plans out there.

The real business plan

1. Elevator pitch
2. Statement of core values
3. 'Market map'
4. List of key customers
5. List of key allies
6. 'Team sheet' – your current people, who they are and what they do
7. Sales plan
8. Delivery plan. How these sales will be delivered
9. People plan. Who is going to do what. If you need to hire new people in, what sort of people and when. How will everyone's delivery against the people plan be measured.
10. Financial projections

If you have a part-time FD by now, they will be the architect of the plan. If you haven't, then try getting an MBA student to help (avoid the arrogant ones). If they click with you and the team, they may come and join you. Bright, enthusiastic young people are what you will need in the next stage of the company's growth.

Some of the terms in the plan are self-explanatory or have already been explained.Here are some comments on the others.

Statement of core values

The elevator pitch says what you are going to do; this is about the spirit in which you intend to do it. You have to mean it, of course. We have become cynical faced with empty corporate mission statements, but the start-up can and should live by its values.

Keep the list short. Three or four? Your main source of these values is yourself. Entrepreneur and foil in particular, hopefully cornerstones too.

Some people may think this is all a bit worthy, but I believe values pay off in the long term, even if they may rule out some courses of action that appear to bring short-term benefit. As I've said, much business is based on trust – a by-product of operating by values. Another benefit is in motivation once you start taking on staff. The sort of people you want in your dream team – bright, able, positive – aren't just there for the money but want to feel they are contributing to something of value.

Market map

Sit down with the team and think about this one. Who are your main competitors, and why are you different from them? Make your answers visual. This is best worked out using a whiteboard. I find a graph with an x and y axis on it a helpful way of doing this. Experiment with different values on the axes. Cost and quality are two classic ones. 'We're a lot cheaper than ABC, but they offer all sorts of add-ons.' 'We're much higher quality than XYZ, though they undercut us on price.'

Use different values. Levels of expertise. Geographical reach. When Martin and Andy Dawson were developing Broker's Gin, one of the axes was 'masculine' versus 'feminine' taste. They'd been in the business and knew exactly what this meant.

List of key customers

List your favourite customer organisations, and your favourite people within them. I suggest a dozen names, but if more people really do love you and what you do, put them on there.

Also include a list of key *potential* customers, prospects you would like to see on your list, and what your plans are for attracting them.

List of key allies

Small businesses can create win–win situations with larger organisations if they think it through and put in some effort.

Is there a trade body? Can you be active in it in some way? These can consume time, but you can learn a lot about your market, how it works, and most important, who the movers and shakers are, by getting involved.

Technology businesses may find themselves involved in strategic partnerships. This can take a number of forms. Strategic partners can help out with facilities, funding or expertise. If they think your technological expertise will give them a competitive advantage, then this makes sense for them. In the software/high-tech industry, the best strategic partners are manufacturers, not service companies. The logo of a big service provider might look good on your website, but they can drop alliances very quickly.

List the influencers in your network. Have another list of influencers you intend to get on your side.

In this section, you should also list your trusted advisers on key subjects (HR, law, etc).

Team sheet

'Our people are our greatest asset' is a mantra intoned by many businesses. Some of them actually mean it. Beermat businesses definitely mean it.

List your people in your plan: who they are, what they do now and how they intend to embrace future responsibilities as the business expands.

The plans (sales, delivery, people) and the financials

These are pretty self-explanatory. Sales forecasts must be backed up by evidence. Is your sales funnel in good shape? If you say you will double sales next year, precisely how are you going to do that?

Arguably, the people plan is the most important part of the whole document.

Having your finance cornerstone in charge of writing your real business plan is essential. They will keep it grounded.

Premises

The business often finds itself in need of proper, permanent premises at this time. They'll still be pretty simple, but they'll be yours.

Simple is good, anyway. Clients visiting your premises don't want to come away thinking they are funding a luxury lifestyle. They want to see commitment, energy and excitement, not fish tanks and Axminster carpets. I actually worked with an entrepreneur who insisted on having a tank of piranhas in reception. And yes, he more than once 'entertained' clients by chucking a goldfish into the tank.

Accessible is good too. Near public transport (the tube if you're in London) and, especially outside London, with places to park.

Since *The Beermat Entrepreneur* was first published, the office supply business has changed radically for the better. The old Wild-West system of dingy premises, dodgy estate agents and endless hassles getting phones (let alone internet access) installed has largely been replaced by incubators and nice, flexible serviced offices. Shop around, find one you like and move in.

One caveat. Avoid schemes that offer you office space, or office space plus 'support' (which often means people trying to sell you consultancy), for equity.

Make the move special. Take photographs of the first day. Crack open a bottle of something.

To me, this marks *the end of the seedling phase*. There's a huge psychological power to the company having an office, where people have to turn up to work at (reasonably) regular times, and where business is the focus – unlike working from home where there are always distractions. You interact more. Ideas get kicked around. You get a much deeper understanding of, and (hopefully) connection to, your fellow team members. If the business is to thrive, you will have to gel into a team, taking on the world. Sharing physical space is a very important part of this.

Another version of this milestone is when you take on your first full-time employee, which often happens around the same time, but I prefer the 'premises' one.

The intrapreneur

The intrapreneur, the entrepreneur who does it from inside the big company, has many advantages over the entrepreneur going it alone. Premises? You have an office already. Materials? There will be extra stuff lying around somewhere. Distribution and manufacturing facilities will be available if you know where to look.

The intrapreneur needs to be a brilliant networker, with contacts in all parts of the company. Through this network, they will know when a machine is idle, a programmer at a loose end, some materials sitting in a corner left over from a production run. Does a department have some budget that they need to spend by next month or they won't get allocated so much next year?

It really helps to be a magnet. The intrapreneur needs to be able to charm the machinist, the programmer, the budget holder.

Like an entrepreneur, they need to find a mentor high in the company – right at the top if possible. An in-house corporate mentor is often referred to as a 'sponsor'. The sponsor can help in all the ways a mentor helps an entrepreneur 'out there', but has an extra role, too, a political one, batting for the intrapreneur within the company (a process often referred to as championing).

This is great – but intrapreneurs shouldn't just leave the politics to their mentor. They have to form their own alliances. They have to know who their enemies are too. There will be people who are jealous because the project is going well, or who consider it wasteful if it isn't going well, or who simply don't like fancy new stuff being done in the hallowed space of the company. Intrapreneurs have to navigate round such people. Their sponsor can help, but intrapreneurs need political nous too.

In other ways, the intrapreneur simply has to follow the same rules as the entrepreneur. Above all, they must build a team around them. A foil and cornerstones, individuals within the company with the necessary core skills who really believe in and will put time into the new product. The team must be incentivised. One big disadvantage the intrapreneur has over the entrepreneur is that they do not have chunks of equity to offer. The main incentives they can offer instead are a more fun, a less corporate working environment and that old corporate goody of status within the company. 'There goes Karim. He was one of the team behind the magic widget.'

Intrapreneurship is not easy, but if you are imaginative, good at human relations and savvy, with a bit of a taste for intrigue (though *not* for intrigue for its own sake), then it can be a great adventure.

Time to celebrate!

Remember that evening in the pub? So much has happened since then.

You got that first customer and delighted them. You got more customers. You slowly realised that a huge area of pain was not being solved by you or anyone else and moved into that area. You have begun to get a reputation for excellence in that area. You have a mentor on board who has already opened a number of important doors for you. You recently hired a part-time finance director. Just as well, as you had to negotiate an increased bank overdraft last week, as new, bigger orders are coming in (the company has no other debt, having paid off the initial bank loan a few months ago).

These new orders are largely from what have become regulars, customers who love what you deliver and want more. The founding team remains solid, respecting each other's skills, and getting ever better at these skills as they put them into practice. The real business plan you recently drew up looks both optimistic and achievable. And you've just moved into your own office.

Celebrate all this. Extravagantly. Why not? You are also allowed to mingle a little sadness with your celebration. As the business gets into a new gear – as the seedling grows taller than one metre – it changes its nature. Once you start taking people on to deliver against your real business plan, the glory days will be over – the days of you, the founders, against the world. Shame, in a way. Business may never be quite as much fun. But the future is beckoning.

The business is no longer a seedling, but a sapling.

The adventure continues.

The sapling enterprise

The next phase of the life of your business, the 'sapling', covers the period when it grows from the founding team to a business with around 25 people on board.

Why 25? I have no idea, but I discovered it to be another magic number, like 5. At The Instruction Set the whole nature of the company changed after we grew beyond 25. It turned from a tribe into a machine almost overnight. I have seen the same happen in many other businesses since.

I know that not every business undergoes this change at exactly 25. But many do so at this figure or at a figure oddly close it. I don't know why. Others manage to keep the tribal thing going longer, but not forever. The key thing to understand is that it will happen, however hard you work at keeping things tribal. It will happen quickly and suddenly and unexpectedly, and it will come with a sense of loss.

Note that the key dividing line between the two phases is the number of people in the company, not turnover, profitability or any fancy business ratio. It's another indicator of that profound truth that business is fundamentally about people.

Many businesses choose to stop growing around this level, aware perhaps of impending bureaucratisation if they grow any further. Juliet Price has kept Park City Consulting this size and loves what she calls the 'family atmosphere'. Such a business is often called a boutique. It serves a niche market, its customers come by personal recommendation (and come *back*, again and again). Its style is personal, friendly, deeply committed. Everyone in the business shares the vision and is prepared to put in the hours and effort to realise it. Nobody hides behind a job spec: if something needs doing they do it.

Other entrepreneurs take the plunge and grow further – more on this later.

The sapling phase is a special time. Make sure you take plenty of team photographs along the way. At The Instruction Set we took pictures of every person as they joined, and had them pinned up in a 'rogues gallery' in the office, along with a brief description of what they did and an employee number, a bit like a football shirt, based on when they joined.

The top team

I've already stated my preference for a five-person team to run the sapling business. Two people are a marriage. Three people are a marriage plus an outsider. Four people are two marriages. This may sound silly, but groups of four so often split into two feuding individuals watched by two others, who either look on with disappointment or take sides. The Beatles, still my favourite band, were a sad example of this, falling apart once their manager Brian Epstein died.

Five just seems to be the number that works. It's big enough for flexibility, for grouping and regrouping of individuals round different ideas at different times. It's too small for cliques to form within it. And it's odd, so a majority vote can always be taken.

What should the five-person team look like? My ideal line-up is:

- **The entrepreneur**: The person with the vision, the ultimate passion and the charisma. The boss.
- **The delivery cornerstone**: The person in charge of processes and procedures.
- **The sales cornerstone**: No revenue, no business!
- **The finance cornerstone**: Not expert at flashy high finance, but at cash management, cost control, financial planning and managing relationships with capital providers and other professionals.
- **A fifth person**: The one I call the 'critical factor cornerstone'.

One of the four cornerstones, remember, will also be the foil, now playing their dual role.

The critical factor cornerstone

This person is closely connected with what makes and keeps your business special. They ensure it stays ahead of the game. In a technology-driven business, this is usually the technical innovator.

In a software house, the technical innovator is writing early versions of the idea, up to 1.0. This version breaks all the rules, solving pressing problems in an amazing and new way, but probably doesn't actually work. The delivery cornerstone then takes over, improving piecemeal – Versions 1.1, 1.2, 1.3 – until a saleable product is created. While the deliverer is doing this, the innovator starts pulling the whole thing to bits and radically rethinking it to create Version 2.0, which will do more wonderful things but keeps falling over.

In a manufacturing business, the technical innovator's skill is about design, function, construction, materials application, while the delivery cornerstone concentrates on processes, machinery, manning, cost efficiency and materials handling.

Technical innovators ignore resource constraints. For them, anything goes, as long as it creates the new, ground-breaking product. The deliverer, by contrast, has to accept all existing constraints and get the job done within those constraints. Yes, this can lead to tension, but it is a useful and creative one, not just another spat.

For lower-tech businesses there will be a critical, and often very specialised, area of expertise, mastery of which can give you a real edge. For a retail business, for example, the input of someone who is an expert on location can be of immense value. If you are selling FMCG , an expert at the marketing of such products will be essential – though it is a big mistake to think that this removes the need for sales skills. The big retail accounts on which successful FMCG activity is based have to be hunted then farmed.

The entrepreneur

The entrepreneur must always be looking at the bigger picture. Their job is to keep the flame of the business vision ablaze, both internally and when presenting the company to outsiders – to the media and potential customers. They are also the strategist, the grand planner, or at least initiator of grand plans – the other cornerstones will fill in the details.

As the company grows, the entrepreneur will probably still initiate some sales or do bits of technical work, but needs to pass the core responsibility for these areas to the cornerstones.

Supposing the entrepreneur has unique knowledge in the critical factor? This is a tough call. Some delegation will be necessary, otherwise they will burn out.

Administration

Who should be in charge of basic admin? It can be the delivery cornerstone, but I think the best person for the job is the finance cornerstone. They will have a natural feel for value for money. The worst person is definitely the entrepreneur. If you let them loose in this area, you will probably come into the office one morning to find gold taps in the washroom, specially imported papyrus notepaper on everyone's desk, and no milk in the fridge.

Forming the top team

If your founding team is two or three individuals and wishes to move to a full set of five, this means inviting new people into the inner sanctum of the company. This can be a hard ask, and some that founding teams find too difficult.

My advice here is not to rush. Take someone on to do the necessary job and see if they are really up to cornerstone standard, both in the quality of their work and in their passion for the business.

They can be offered small, incremental stakes in the business, but at some point a decision has to be made as to whether they are true cornerstones or simply senior people doing a good job. The existing top team should have a special meeting to discuss this and must be unanimous about granting cornerstone status to someone. If this sounds tricky, my experience is that you know after a while if someone has this magic. It's intuition at work again.

It may be a while before you have your four cornerstones in place – the right four people, with the right skills, commitment and passion for the enterprise. When this happens, your idea will have leapt another hurdle, that of totally convincing four very able people to commit themselves to it.

Management

Once you start taking on people, you and your fellow founders aren't just the business any longer – you're in charge of people. You have to hire staff, to pay them salaries and bonuses, to lead them and motivate them. You have become managers.

> *Help! I wanted to get away from all this boss/underling stuff. All I wanted was to be with a great bunch of mates who believed in this wonderful idea!*

Tough. Some businesses flourish with a close-knit founding team and nobody else. Most don't, especially in services where as demand for your service grows you need ever more people to deliver it. Most ambitious businesses will also need to recruit salespeople, both hunters to do telesales and farmers to manage existing large accounts. A full-time administrator will be needed.

When you have a number of new people – in other words part way through the sapling phase – you will be able to hand over much of their management to a tier of management that you can now afford to bring into the company. More about *sapling managers* later in this chapter.

But to start with, the sapling managers are you.

I recommend going on a short people management course to remind yourselves of the basics. Many business schools and training companies offer these, as does the CIPD (the HR professional body).

Arguably, the most important aspects of management are recruitment, dismissal (hopefully something that won't happen often if you get the first of these right) and appraisal. I shall say a bit about each of these.

Recruitment

This is the most important job at the top of a sapling organisation. Pick the right people and much of the rest will take care of itself.

You are looking to recruit 'dream team' players: passionate and imaginative individuals with a can-do attitude. People who will take initiative, not people who will find reasons for not doing things (there are always good reasons for not doing things). People who don't clock-watch. People without big egos. People with a sense of fun. Team players.

We used a nice, simple acronym for dream-teamers: SWAN. Smart, Work hard, Ambitious (for the company as well as themselves) and Nice.

Juliet Price advises: 'Recruit for passion.'

What you are seeking to avoid, above all, is what former England rugby coach Sir Clive Woodward called 'energy sappers'. Another term for them is 'drains' (as opposed to 'radiators' who spread good vibes). Juliet refers to them as 'terrorists'. Whatever you call them, these individuals leave a trail of confusion behind them, upsetting co-workers. They won't accept responsibility for their own mistakes, always seeking to blame someone else. They question the vision of the company, often adopting a superior tone as if having a vision is childish and stupid. They are the sort of people you come away from talking to feeling upset in some way, but you're not quite sure why. 'What did I say?' Other signs include:

- being rude to 'unimportant' people like the teenager delivering the Friday afternoon pizza
- poor timekeeping
- poor communication
- obsession with status (especially their own)
- long personal calls or lots of time on the internet on irrelevant sites
- dramas, with them at the centre.

The last of these often involve what psychologists call the 'Drama Triangle'. This involves acting out one of three dramatic, attention-grabbing roles: Persecutor, Victim or Rescuer. Other people get roped into these dramas. After all, you can't be a victim without having a horrible persecutor out there. Some drama players add a twist to this, by starting out playing one role then suddenly switching to another. The 'Yes, but . . . ' routine I mentioned in the section on mentoring in Chapter 2: The seedling enterprise is an example of this. One moment you're trying to help someone; the next they are criticising you.

However well qualified for a role an applicant is, do not select them if you or other team members suspect they are energy-sappers (or drains or terrorists). These people need therapy. You need wonderful team members.

Get everyone in the organisation involved in recruitment. Incentivise the bringing in of good people. 'I've got this friend who'd be just perfect for that job. I know they're not happy where they are at the moment.' Brilliant!

A good culture really helps here (more on this below). If your staff think that working for you is the best game in town, they will be eager to get people they like on board. At the same time they will think carefully about who they bring in.

Our meritocratic business ethos frowns on the 'recruiting mates' approach. But for the sapling enterprise, trust and enthusiasm are key qualities, and it is simple common sense to look for those where you would look in ordinary life – among people you know and like. We used this method in the sapling Instruction Set, and created a lively, very diverse company.

The only caveat to the above is to watch out for cronyism by the entrepreneur. Entrepreneurs may try and surround themselves with sycophants – the type you see hanging round celebrities telling them they're cool every ten minutes. The best way to avoid this is to make each director responsible for hiring within their department.

When recruiting to a sapling, give everyone in the company a veto.

Everyone? That's what we did at the sapling Instruction Set, and it worked. Once we decided to take someone on, we introduced them to everyone else in the company. 'Here's Mo. He might be joining us.' If anyone expressed misgivings, we didn't hire. This sounds draconian, but it worked. We built a brilliant, loyal, highly competent dream team. It's the intuition thing again. Trust it.

When you do take people on, make sure they know what you expect them to do. This sounds obvious, but is often overlooked.

The new arrival should be on a trial period. Three months is a good length. Make some time two months into that period to talk with the rest of the top team about this person. Are they fitting in? Are they delivering what they said they would?

After three months, if they are delivering, have 'got' the culture and are living it, have a celebration. If they haven't got the culture and aren't gelling, it's time for them to go. You have to be ruthless about this.

Dismissal

It can also happen that someone appears to be a fit after three months, but 'loses it' later. They have to go too.

Make the separation as amicable as possible. Most sapling enterprises operate in quite small business areas, and you don't want enemies out there gunning for you. Also, friendly dismissal is in keeping with the sapling's tribal atmosphere of trust. There may be legal issues too (see below).

Make the process open and unambiguously fair. There are two main reasons for dismissal of established dream-team members: poor performance and misconduct. In both cases, there are correct procedures to follow. When someone has to go because of poor performance, then there should be a clearly understood pathway, which forms part of the appraisal process. For misconduct, staff should get a verbal warning, then a written warning, before being dismissed.

The most difficult dismissal is of someone who has the right attitude and ability but has been underperforming due to circumstances beyond their control. A partner or child has a life-threatening illness or the individual is hit by illness or depression. The first thing to do is to try and get help for them. Try and adapt their workload to fit. If this doesn't work, there may have to be an agreed parting of the ways, at least temporarily.

When you dismiss a dream-teamer, explain to them that they have not achieved what was hoped. Run through the formal aspects (warnings, missed targets). Ask them if they really feel at home in their work. They may well be very honest about this, as they are secretly feeling guilty for letting the rest of the tribe down. Then break the bad news. Offer a severance package if they've been with you a long time. Avoid personal criticism.

Have someone in the top team who does the firing. You need someone likeable and with a reputation for fairness and total integrity. The finance cornerstone is often the best person to do this. Dave Griffiths had this job at The Instruction Set. In a perfect world, the entrepreneur would do this, but many entrepreneurs can get too emotional at a time which needs calm.

Some businesses have 'corporate Rottweilers' to do this job. You can guess my view on this. Be grown-up enough to do the job yourself and to do it properly.

Ideally, there should be a second meeting, the exit interview, a while later. The person leaves, takes a break, comes to terms with what has happened, then comes back to tie up any loose ends. Agree to differ on any contentious points. Finalise severance agreements. Keep the parting as amicable as possible.

Some enlightened companies try to find jobs for ex-employees. Accenture does this, with the result that it has friends in high places all over the business world.

Enter the consultant

The legal side of employment can be tricky – and is perpetually changing. The law currently says that you can dismiss people in a pretty summary manner for up to two years after they are taken on. You, of course, will be nicer than that. However, there is a catch. Under the Equality Act of 2010 you can face legal action if the person who has been dismissed can prove they have been discriminated against on a range of grounds: gender, race, belief, sexual orientation or disability. You don't do stuff like that – you're an ethical Beermat business – but a disappointed ex-employee may think otherwise. Disability includes mental disability, which can be a grey area.

I suggest employing an HR consultant. Ask around for a good one and do a good deal with them - you're a growing company and if you like them, there'll be plenty of work in the future. They can draft basic offer letters and contracts. They can put correct procedures in place and keep you updated with the law. If for some reason, a disgruntled ex-employee does try to sue you, a good HR consultant can be hugely valuable.

Many litigants vanish once they get a cost estimate from their lawyers. But having a pro on your side will also help scare these destructive people off.

The whole business of contracts, HR procedures and so on may seem contrary to the 'anything goes' spirit of the sapling. But 'anything' doesn't go in the sapling. Clear rules and boundaries are set, within which people then have freedom.

The case of the crumbling cornerstone

It can happen that one of the cornerstones stops pulling their weight during the sapling phase. They looked good to start with. When you had your equity meeting, the team agreed that they were doing a good job and were worth their early stake. But things have changed.

Sales cornerstones can run out of energy. They keep on being asked to increase revenue, and simply can't.

Technical cornerstones may find it stressful that other, often younger technical people are now in the team and will sometimes disagree with them (and, even more annoying, will sometimes be right). Back in the good old seedling days, their word on technical matters was law. This can demotivate them at a time when they need to be supercharging their motivation.

Any cornerstone might find their new role as a people manager stressful. Some cornerstones take to management like ducks to water as they are good with people and logically minded. Others don't.

As always, a prompt reaction is needed. Entrepreneurial businesses cannot afford passengers, even ones who once added great value. The rest of the top team must get together and sort things out.

Sit the cornerstone down and talk things through with them. There's always a hope that they can get back on track, especially if the problem is addressed quickly and robustly. Otherwise, there are various solutions.

It can be possible to find a new role for the crumbling cornerstone. Technical innovators will probably relish the chance of running some kind of skunkworks. Who knows? They might be like Steve Jobs and end up saving the company. Maybe they'll be even more like Steve Jobs and do that twice.

If the cornerstone is crumbling under the stress of their new people management role, consider getting a *sapling manager* in to take this job away from them. As the business grows, you will be introducing these people anyway. Maybe now is the time.

I hated sales management, and after a while, we hired someone to manage both the young, eager hunter salespeople and the more experienced account-managing farmers we were bringing on board. My roles became hunting for bigger business and making regular visits to the sales team to chat to them and generally spread positive vibes. I would also sometimes go with them to tricky or big customers. I remained ultimately responsible for revenue. If that faltered, I was the one in the firing line at the board meeting.

We had two technical experts in our top team. Neither really wanted to manage the business of delivering training. So, once revenue allowed, we got someone to do that job. One of the cornerstones worked on a parallel software project, the other kept the courses bang up to date and wrote new ones. Both also would give courses when required. They also acted as inspiration for younger, less knowledgeable 'makers' in the company.

Even our finance cornerstone, who was the best people manager of all of us, ended up with his own financial manager. Dave kept the crucial jobs of sustaining relationships with the bank, of staying aware of the market for potential funding (even though we never actually tapped it, it was important we knew what possibilities were around) and of looking at the financial implications of various possible future courses of action. He was also the foil, remember, discussing big picture stuff *à deux* with the entrepreneur. The financial manager did the less glamorous stuff like VAT, management accounts, insurance and basic admin.

The people you bring in to manage in sapling businesses are, like cornerstones, special. Like cornerstones, they combine some professional skill with a sense of adventure. Their move to you can often be slightly left-field. Our financial manager came from an accountancy practice, not from the finance department of another business – there's a huge difference between those two environments. Our delivery manager was an academic, initially hired part-time to present training courses, who fancied a change of scene. He never went back to academia and went on to a very successful management career.

Sapling managers may have management responsibility but they are still, above all, dream team members. Work is an adventure for them, not just another step up a ladder. They'll be pushing their boundaries and enjoying doing so. Like the rest of the dream team, they won't hide behind job specs. Our delivery manager still went out and gave courses when we needed him to.

But back to the crumbling cornerstone. If, despite having a sapling manager take away work they dislike, they are still turning into passengers – a sales cornerstone no longer getting business, or a technical innovation cornerstone no longer innovating – they will have to go.

Their departure must be handled with tact and fairness. The leaver will usually expect the company to buy back their equity stake, as they will at some level have lost their faith in the business. But if for some reason they need to leave but still believe (for example, if they quit for personal reasons), I believe they should be allowed to keep their stake, or at least part of it, and cash it in big time when the company gets massive. They've earned it.

If the stake is bought back, it is the finance cornerstone's job to assess how much it is worth. This assessment might be queried by the crumbling cornerstone (or, of course, the finance cornerstone may *be* the crumbling one). During the dotcom era a useful formula for valuing a business was the number of MBAs in the organisation, times the number of incomprehensible buzzwords in the mission statement, times £10 million. To me a business is worth the amount of cash you have in the bank plus the value of the next three months' orders. The truth no doubt lies in between.

This is one of the many times your mentor will be of great use. Have them oversee this process and let them suggest a fair pay-out.

Avoid the case ending up in court, both at the time and also later, by making the parting agreement legally watertight.

If you are a cornerstone who has crumbled, don't be ashamed. You were tested to your limits, which is a great privilege. Most people spend their working lives safely within their boundaries, quietly battling on but in some deep way dissatisfied. You did different. Appreciate this.

Accept the mentor's or FD's assessment of your parting value.

As well as crumbling under pressure, a cornerstone might simply find themselves no longer fitting. A loose cornerstone perhaps. When they joined the company, they thought we were going to do x. Now we're doing y. This was a running debate at The Instruction Set, where we originally planned to write world-beating software and use training as a cash cow to fund that, but ended up concentrating on the training. We always managed to keep things together, but I've seen other businesses that haven't, where a change of direction has made one or some of the founders irrelevant.

As usual, the issue must be addressed. If the loose cornerstone really wants to do x, and you can't find a skunkworks-type role where they can do that, then set them free to go off and do it themselves, as entrepreneurs running their own business. Do so in a positive way, wishing them well, and offering assistance where possible (not financial, but via recommendation and occasional advice).

The departure of a cornerstone is rarely easy. As the founding team of a seedling business that has already made it to fast-growing sapling, you were a band of brothers, sisters or siblings. The emotional wrench of splitting such a band can be considerable. But it has to be done.

A foil can also crumble at this stage. They might have a bigger stake. This can be problematic, especially in businesses where there were two founders with equal, or nearly equal, stakes. It's too late to just walk away and start the business up again, but you can't keep them as a passenger either.

There's no easy remedy for this. They have to be bought out, and the process can be incredibly draining. If you have a mentor, use them. Make sure that you keep your attention on the business while this issue is getting sorted out. And don't give up. Once the dead-weight foil has gone, the business usually gets a new lease of life.

Appraisal

But let's stay positive. You've got great people. However, you still need to keep checking that they are doing their job and are happy about that. The top team needs appraisal too, so have regular meetings to discuss your own performance.

The best appraisal is invisible and ongoing. The entrepreneur or the relevant cornerstone is regularly stopping for a brief chat with the dream-teamer to find out how they feel things are going. Make notes after these chats.

Formal appraisal should happen every six months. It must be person-to-person. Every team member sits down with their manager and looks at what they have done in that six months, at what they can learn from it and at what the manager expects from them in the next six months. Targets need to be set.

At the same time, it's a good opportunity for the manager to get some feedback about how they are perceived and to talk to the individual about the company in general.

If someone fails to meet the targets set six months ago, the best question is 'What do we need to help you get it right next time?' This is an infinitely better question than an accusatory 'Why?', which just puts people on the defensive. Proper dream-teamers will usually tell you what they need.

If you're not convinced by their answer, spend time with them. The sales cornerstone should go with an under-performing salesperson on a visit and try to spot what they are doing wrong. It will often be something very obvious. If so, stay cool, point out the error (after the sales meeting, of course) and let them learn from the experience. The same is true of technical staff. Get the relevant cornerstone to spend some time working alongside them, to see what they're doing wrong, and then help them sort it out.

If there's an individual that you and the rest of the team really like, and who loves the company, but who is underperforming in their current role, then consider if they might be of use elsewhere in the business. You are well shot of energy-sapping mediocrity and cynicism, but passion that hasn't yet found its best medium of expression is unrefined gold. Work on it.

Thanks, but I'm off

We lost very few dream-teamers in The Instruction Set. But that was a while ago. 21st century millennials can be more footloose. They do gel, they do really get the business, but somehow some other goal is calling and off they go. Accept this and wish them well.

Especially in the service sector, watch out for former employees taking your good wishes too seriously and starting rival companies. Restrictive covenants in initial contracts can help, but there's no substitute for getting a farmer on the case straightaway and talking to all the customers the deserter might try and poach.

If the boot is on the other foot, and you are planning to leave and set up on your own, act ethically. Don't just set up a carbon copy of the business you have just left. You're more imaginative than that. Don't poach customers unless you feel they were being appallingly treated by your old employer.

While I despair of organisations with high staff turnover, a gentle turnover can be beneficial. New people bring new ideas, new contacts, a slightly new vibe.

Leadership

Even when it can hand over the day-to-day management of people to sapling managers, the top team still has the job of *leading* them. The most important ways you do this are by creating the culture of the business and by motivating people. A third function of leadership – much beloved in business schools – is strategy. Some thoughts on these . . .

Culture

Culture is a deep thing. It's about identity – proper, felt-inside personal identity, not vague, plastered-on corporate identity. What kind of person is a Your Company Person? Your Company People will do things a certain way, have expectations of what's acceptable and what isn't, value certain things and be repelled by certain other things. It's about belonging.

Your business will have a culture, whether you want it to or not, as people in groups form common standards. You can either lead the process of culture formation or let it happen in a haphazard way. No prizes for guessing which option I recommend.

The best one for sapling enterprises is tribal. Think chiefs and warriors (modern chiefs and warriors can be female as easily as male). Think close personal relationships. Make the company a place where everyone knows everyone else well. Make sure they all get on.

Laundry Republic gets a cake in for each employee's birthday, and every team member who is on the premises comes down to see it presented to them and to sing Happy Birthday. Work anniversaries are also celebrated. Recently one was missed and founder Ian Walker insisted a bottle of Champagne be given to the individual.

Lead by example. As with culture formation, you can't not do this. People will imitate you. So lead by conscious example, in your actions, reactions, expectations, comments, mood. You cannot hide behind spreadsheets or technology.

Building a tribe of 25 people who are both excellent at their work and who get on socially isn't easy. 'You have to work at it all the time,' says MiddletonMurray founder Angela Middleton. But it can also be fun – and should be. Be inventive and enjoy being inventive.

At The Instruction Set, we would all go down to the pub most Friday nights. This may seem a little *passé* nowadays, but I urge you to do something similar: a meal, bowling, something where you all do enjoyable stuff together. It was great fun and I still miss it. Sometimes, the session was totally unstructured, with the only rule that the top team buys the first round and continues to be generous thereafter. Other times we had awards. These awards were, of course, very informal, though behind the informality a lot of thought had gone into who got the awards and why.

There were three basic ones. 'Mini Oscars' went to people who had done particularly special things that month – won a big contract, solved some particularly nagging technical problem, had been particularly praised by a client (or whatever). There was a 'Pranny of the Month' award for some mild balls-up like locking yourself out of your car or spilling coffee all over a report. 'Unsung Hero' usually went to someone quite junior and rather introverted who'd done something special.

These may sound a bit juvenile, like giving stickers to small children, but, believe me, they worked (in a company that wasn't just a bunch of blokes but diverse). The rather serious accounts assistant glowed with pride on being nominated Pranny of the Month. Suddenly they had the right not to be so earnest, so quietly, dully perfect. The systems administrator – one of those jobs where you only get noticed when things go wrong – really did appreciate their Unsung Hero award.

These informal get-togethers are also good places to spot potential dissent. However good your hiring and culture management, dissenting cliques will spring up occasionally. These need to be nipped in the bud, not by firing dissenters but by talking to the individuals involved and getting to the bottom of what their problem is. Are there three people sitting in one corner, backs turned towards the rest of the team? It sounds obvious, but I've seen it.

Office romances may become more apparent in informal settings. These spring up a lot in sapling enterprises. It's a sign that the culture is working that people are really getting close. Go ahead and celebrate them – with the obvious proviso that the participants' work mustn't suffer.

I'm talking about romances between equals, of course. I know of companies where senior people have abused their position to pursue subordinates, and it is very damaging to tribe morale. If you, as a top team member, really do decide that the accounts assistant is the love of your life, then that person will have to leave the firm. If you just fancy a casual fling, go and take a cold shower.

Formal team-building exercises can help build culture too. One that I found particularly useful was role-swapping. Get the techies to meet clients. Send the sales staff on a technical course. Efficiency experts might throw up their clipboards in horror at this, but the more everyone in the sapling tribe understands and appreciates what everyone else does, the better that business will run.

I actually think that our cheerful, intense, essentially caring culture was a key, maybe the key, to our success. Our product was good, but once people started to copy it, it was arguably not that much better than any-one else's. We worked hard, and pretty smart, but so do most start-ups. Our culture and our people were utterly outstanding – and that culture grew in our sapling period and was lived by our sapling dream team.

Motivation

It could be argued that this section belongs earlier, where I talk about management. Isn't that the manager's job? Not in a sapling. Even when the company is big enough to have a tier of 'sapling management', it is the chief's job to motivate all the tribe. Other senior figures should help of course.

I've worked a lot in sapling organisations over the years – I prefer them to large organisations – and I have a sense of what drives dream team people.

Purpose. The dream team all appreciate the point of the company – its core values. They're not just there to get paid and make money for the shareholders.

Participation. Many dream-teamers come from big organisations where they have felt swamped and irrelevant. They want to be involved in the making of decisions, and they want to know that their decisions and actions have real consequences.

Respect. This is both self- and peer respect. They like the people they work with. They respect their colleagues and are respected by them. Outside working hours, they tell their friends they are working for your company and expect those friends to be impressed and even envious.

Challenge. Sapling employees are there for a challenge – to stretch them-selves, to learn and grow. There is plenty of opportunity for this in sapling businesses as there are always more things to do than people to do them. So if anyone has the guts to say 'Let me try', unless it's obviously inap-propriate, congratulate them on their initiative and let them.

Flexibility. Modern dream-teamers want to weave their working lives in with their personal lives. They want to work more flexible hours. Can they work from home at all?

What of those old motivators, career advancement, security and, of course, money? They still matter a bit.

Advancement. Life in a sapling enterprise is more about the challenge of the job than getting vice-president on your business card. But there will be opportunities for advancement if the sapling grows into a mighty oak, and some people join sapling organisations with this in mind.

Security is rather despised by the young go-getters who join sapling enterprises, but note that older employees start worrying about it. Older people can be very valuable in sapling teams, so bear this change of priority in mind.

Money always matters. It can be particularly important initially to attract good people. Ian Walker of Laundry Republic points out that if you offer above the market rate, you not only get the best people but widen the range of possible individuals interested in a job. 'I'd not really seen myself as an x, but if they're paying £y for it, I'll give it a go.'

Pay well and give bonuses too. But not individual bonuses – whatever any books on management or experts you meet in pubs tell you. It simply isn't true that you can pay staff wildly different amounts of money and nobody will find out. People will find out, and the discovery of huge differentials will breed arrogance or demotivation. Individual bonuses go against the tribal culture that drives sapling enterprises. You are all in this together, remember? Team bonuses are good things – given to everyone, based on the performance of the tribe as a whole.

I don't like sales commissions either. Yes, have a lively, competitive atmosphere in the sales department, but keep that fun. We had a daily sales chart on the wall called the Greedometer, which we half took seriously and half poked fun at ourselves for taking seriously.

I believe that everyone's salary and bonuses should be public knowledge. The sort of people you want to employ in sapling organisations aren't irrationally envious. They're quite happy for someone to be earning £200,000, provided they think that person is adding an appropriate amount of value to the team effort. Post salaries on the company intranet. Why not? If anyone comes and asks why they are underpaid, explain why, and most important what they have to do to get paid better. And if your £200,000 person is clearly useless – I've worked with people getting twice this amount, who seemed to bring nothing to the party at all – then the more embarrassed and humiliated they feel at this, the better.

Such a policy encourages openness. It discourages overgenerous golden hellos to people (often pals of the entrepreneur).

I'm against the current fashion for unpaid internships. Yes, it saves you money in the short term, but it's disrespectful and thus bad for morale. Either people are dream-teamers, passionately committed to the company, or they're not. You want full commitment from day one. Why should somebody give this to you if you think so little of them that you won't even pay them properly? I also happen to think it's morally wrong not to pay people for work.

Get apprentices instead. MiddletonMurray (www.middletonmurray .com) runs an excellent scheme.

Set up a stock option system for staff. I say more about this in Chapter 4: The mighty oak.

The Beermat guide to dream team needs

- Purpose
- Participation
- Respect
- Challenge
- Flexibility
- Advancement
- Security
- Money (of course)

What do you actually do to get the best out of people who are motivated in this way?

Some time after The Instruction Set had been sold, I did some work with Insights Ltd, a company run by Will Carling, a former England rugby captain. He and a few chosen sportsmen and sportswomen made a good business out of applying lessons and techniques from professional sport to the workplace.

The tribal sapling enterprise is the ideal place to use these. The number of people involved is about the same as a sports team. The mindset of sapling employees – even ones who hate sport – is similar to that of most sports participants. Young at heart, energetic, up for a challenge. Sapling business is a team game in a way that the seedling isn't (too small), and the larger business, despite efforts at team-building, can never be. There really are only a handful of you, and it's you against the world. And it's bloody marvellous, believe me.

The great sports leaders motivate their players in a number of ways.

Understanding the individual

Sportspeople may all seem super-competent, but they actually vary wildly in temperament. Some are plagued with lack of confidence. It's their undeservedly low self-image that keeps them practising and practising. Others have booming, overconfident egos. Success comes to them because they know it will. Out on the field it may not be clear which person has which self-image. Give them the wrong kind of motivation and it becomes apparent at once.

It's an old story now, but I still love the example that Will quoted of Mike Brearley, one of England's greatest cricket captains. He led England to victory in the historic 1981 Headingley Test by bowling out Australia, who needed a mere 130 to win, for 111. The man who did the damage was Bob Willis. After a brief, unsuccessful spell bowling up the slight slope at the ground, Willis asked to change ends. Brearley ribbed him about this, implying he was getting old, but let him change. Suitably wound up, Willis tore through the Australian batting.

Other team members required totally different motivation. Apparently tough, no-nonsense Yorkshireman Geoff Boycott needed regular reassurance. Ultra-competitive star turn Ian Botham needed to know the skipper wasn't trying to rival him. Derek Underwood, a technically minded spin bowler, needed a lot of listening to and consultation about the details of tactics.

No two individuals' motivation buttons are the same, and it is the job of the leader to know exactly where the ones are for each member of their team.

It is interesting to speculate how many people who appear to be under-performers are actually people whom nobody has taken the trouble to work out how to motivate. Of course, ideally we should all be self-motivators. If you are an entrepreneur, intrapreneur, foil or cornerstone, you will be.

Not slagging off failure but learning from it

There's no point in getting at people for their failures. If somebody goofs, the need is for them, and the rest of the team, to learn from that mistake.

Blame cultures encourage people to put their own safety before the welfare of the group, to score cheap points off one another, and generally to avoid risk. They encourage an energy-sapper's love of drama. Not what you want in an entrepreneurial business, or a sports team whose job it is to go out and win.

Note that our 'Pranny of the Month' ceremony in the pub was always carefully set up to be in a light, humorous spirit, a spirit of cheerful forgiveness and inclusion rather than of blame and exclusion.

Celebrating success

This gets drilled into sports teams, which is why you see macho Premiership footballers kissing and hugging each other after a goal. Your team achievements should be celebrated too, not just with money but with days out, bottles of Champagne at the office, meals, trips to concerts, movies. You are effectively writing the story of your company's success here, and the more clearly that story is embedded in everybody's minds via happy memories, the better.

Giving praise

Individual success should also be celebrated in public, which multiplies the motivational value of the praise. It's extraordinary how seldom people get praise from some bosses, even when the boss genuinely reckons that the work has been excellent. But there is no better way of motivating people. Giving praise also sends out a general message. This is a place where excellence is encouraged and celebrated. In Britain, we're not very good at this. Good old mediocrity has been the norm. It's important to break down such negativity, and to understand that it does not need to be replaced by selfishness but by positive, enthusiastic teamwork.

Being visible

I've already talked about 'leading by example' as part of culture formation. It is also part of the day-to-day business of motivating the team.

Will Carling told a story of how, just before a crucial game, he was spotted wandering around the team hotel, deep in thought. It wasn't that he was worried, just that he wanted to think of something original to say to his players. Observers misinterpreted this and thought he'd given up on the game. Gloom set in. Until he realised what had happened, Carling was baffled by this sudden change of morale. Once he had spotted the cause, he was able to address the problem. England went on to win.

Visibility is also important in big companies. A similar story to the above comes from Next PLC. The CEO came out of the boardroom one day after excellent reports all round, pondering the next move. As he walked down the corridor, lost in thought, staff spotted his expression and panic set in among them. 'The boss is upset!' 'Something's gone terribly wrong!' 'How many are going to be laid off?' 'Bet you 1,000 . . . ' 'More like 2,000 probably . . . ' Morale nose-dived, and it took a meeting of head office staff to get it back again.

Staying positive

The leader's positivity has to be full-time – whatever is happening in your personal life, or to the company for that matter. This does not mean 'tell lies about the state of the business'. It does mean that if things are looking tough, show the full force of your determination to sort things out.

Generating enthusiasm

This is a job for the entrepreneur, and it really is a gift. You can't learn how to do this really effectively, though like all emotional intelligence skills you can improve those gifts that you have. Entrepreneurs do it naturally, their enthusiasm bubbling out all over the place and their commitment showing that they really mean it.

Leading from the front

Showing you mean it means leading from the front. It means being seen to be working as hard and as smart as your brightest employee. The old-style corporate apparatchik who did a lot of 'work' on the golf course or over a long lunch may well still have a role in a big company – contacts are kept alive this way – but this is not a style that suits the sapling enterprise.

Setting goals

Leaders set goals. Goal-setting is about having a vision of where an individual can get to, and about understanding the steps they have to take to get there. Well-set goals plot a path to success via a series of challenging but achievable milestones. These, of course, then need to be monitored.

Carling used to say that the captain's job is to 'create an environment where people can succeed'.

Strategy

As well as creating the culture and motivating the tribe, the leader has to make sure the business is going in the right direction. However, there is often not too much complex strategic thinking to be done at the sapling stage. It's more about staying on course than amazing new changes of tack. The aim, simply, is to grow via:

- an energetic, happy, motivated team
- carefully controlled costs
- products that consistently delight customers.

And radical innovation? Your product must have been innovative to have got this far, so your thinking should probably be more about building your market rather than disrupting that market again. Continuous improvement rather than radical reinvention is usually the best strategy for the sapling. But keep on your toes. Keep your products fresh, refine them, find new uses and markets for them. Evolve.

Evolution still requires imagination and courage. Paradise Wildlife Park, the zoo just off the M25 north of London, was already a successful small business when it pioneered the idea of animal experiences, where visitors could get involved in the running of the zoo, most notably being 'a keeper for a day', shadowing a keeper as they went about their work. The zoo industry was unimpressed, writing it off as a gimmick. Paradise's customers loved it, the keepers enjoyed it – and now almost every zoo in the country is offering this extra.

When they came up with the new idea, Paradise didn't close down and start again, or open a rival zoo with the new feature. They kept the existing business going and trialled the idea. It worked, so they did more of it. If it hadn't worked, they would have quietly dropped it. Such is most sapling innovation.

Incidentally, I find it intriguing that strategy-speak often resorts to the imagery of war, of giant armies clashing. There's a sub-genre of books that wheel out classic military thinkers, like Sun Zi (Sun Tzu in old-fashioned spelling) or Clausewitz, and reinterpret what they teach for the business market. This may be relevant to great corporations but I believe strongly that the sports field is an infinitely better metaphor and inspiration for the sapling business.

Sapling sales

Sales drove the seedling business. Without them, it was just a clever idea. This continues to be the case with the sapling.

The sales funnel needs to be regularly topped up and regularly monitored. But most of all, the sapling's existing clients need to be attended to and loved. It's an old piece of business wisdom that 80% of profits come from 20% of your customers. This idea originated with the 19th century sociologist Wilfredo Pareto, who was also a keen gardener and noticed that 80% of the peas he harvested came from 20% of his pods. Pareto then extended this principle to other matters, including wealth distribution in his native Italy, and the concept has been spreading ever since.

It's not always 80/20 for the seedling, but as the business settles down and begins to become known and trusted in its market, things often end up that way (or around that figure). So be *very* nice to that 20%.

It helps to know who the 20% are. This sounds flip, but it's amazing how many small businesses don't actually know how much profit they make from each customer. Your finance cornerstone or finance manager should provide this information.

Attending to them is farming work, not hunting. The sales cornerstone is a hunter by nature, and must be kept on this job, looking to open new doors. You need to take on farmer salespeople, account managers, to do this work. It helps if these people are magnets, but they don't have to be hugely powerful ones. Good farmers are thoughtful, affable, good listeners. They are methodical. They stay in regular but un-pushy touch with their contacts, via social media and regular personal visits.

The farmers must be listened to within the company. Your sales cornerstone is your senior salesperson. They have earned this seniority but they mustn't be allowed to hog the sales budget, spending it all on wooing potential new customers. A wise sales cornerstone knows they must avoid doing this, but potential new business can be *soooo* tempting. The board as a whole needs to keep an eye on sales expenditure and ensure that a healthy amount goes to keeping existing customers happy.

Life can out-Pareto Pareto, and present the sapling business with one giant opportunity. One customer that is a) very big and b) loves you so much that it can't get enough of your product. This kind of mega-break – more Jack's Beanstalk than Pareto's pea pods – can propel the sapling to mighty oak status. It is the story behind a lot of successful businesses.

In the ideal scenario, your 'Beanstalk' customer will help you grow, letting you roll out the offer they want so much at a practicable pace.

In a much less ideal scenario, it can turn into a disaster, as you become reliant on that one customer, and thus reliant on the internal politics of that customer, over which you have absolutely no control. If a new CEO arrives with a different vision, you could be out on your ear. Out comes the axe, down comes the Beanstalk, and you are in big trouble.

If possible, when you do a big, potentially business-changing Beanstalk deal, get some kind of termination clause written into the contract. The client can pull out of the deal at any time, without explanation, but they have to pay you a decent amount of money for six months.

Have a Plan B as well. Don't just sit back and say 'Megacorp are buying shedloads of our stuff, we're rich.' Think about who else you could sell to.

Most Beanstalk customers will be understanding. Emma Killilea got her first deal from Sainsbury's, and discussed this with them. They said they realised that as a start-up she would need to be looking to serve other customers as well. They did not ask for exclusivity. They did expect excellent service, and got it.

There's a strategic decision to be made when formulating your Plan B. Do you try and conquer a market? If you're selling loads of your new vegan ready-meals to Waitrose, do you make overtures to Tesco (and, by extension, all the other supermarkets in turn)? Or do you find customers in different markets? Do you start talking to mass caterers and big restaurant chains? A quick rule of thumb is that if you are selling goods go for the former, and if you are selling services go for the latter. But this is far too complex a decision to make by rules of thumb.

As always, talk to your mentor.

Note that if your Beanstalk customer really loves what you do, so much so that they won't let you supply anyone else, consider selling your company to them. It may not be the vast pay-out you dreamt of, but it should be a tidy sum. I talk more about knowing when to sell in Chapter 4: The mighty oak.

By contrast to the potentially wonderful Beanstalk, you will also acquire a number of customers who lose you money, or just about break even but cause a lot of hassle. Here, a decision needs to be made. Sometimes it's worth keeping a foot in the door of a large organisation or an interesting-looking sector. But usually, these people are best let go.

With simply unprofitable customers, up their prices. Get the finance cornerstone to work out what a profitable price would be. Then the sales cornerstone has to go to the client and break the bad news. Take the finance cornerstone along too (unless the client is a tiny one), to explain in clear, spreadsheet terms what your cost of sale is and why the new price is justified.

You will get one of two responses. One is a rather sheepish 'Actually we always thought you were rather cheap. Don't go away! Can you offer us a *small* discount on the new price?' The other is outrage. 'How dare you? We had a rival in here the other day who was offering the same service at an even cheaper price than your old one.' Politely wish the latter type of client well, as the rival might underdeliver and they may want you back again. Look into the rival and their offer to see what's going on. Naurally, keep doing business with the first type of respondent.

The hassle creators are best ditched unless they are major customers or ridiculously profitable. If they are major customers, hire a robust, savvy farmer who knows how to deal with such people.

I've seen big customers bully small service providers in all sorts of subtle ways, and it's horrible. Don't let them.

At the same time, I've also seen account managers get lazy, stop bothering with clients, and clients getting difficult as a result. If you have a lot of complaints coming in, who's doing the farming and are they doing it properly?

Sales events

As the business develops a reputation for expertise in its niche, it can begin promoting conferences and seminars. Such events are good general exposure for the company and can be an excellent showcase for particular products, but above all they are perfect places to make new friends, ones that should lead to further sales.

Make sure the events offer real benefits. Get good external speakers and have really useful information on offer. That way people associate you with quality. At the same time, mix in a few favourite customers telling their stories of how you saved them £100,000 or weeks of work.

You can also charge for the event and still get a decent turnout. 100 people is ideal, big enough to make the room look full, but small enough so that you can make sure that someone from the company gets to talk to every delegate.

Start talking about the event on social media at least a month before. Create a hashtag for it on Twitter and, if there are some interesting pictures to post, on Instagram too.

Don't sell at the event, otherwise the next time you organise one you will get seven people turning up.

Keep it brief. Half a day is long enough for most people's attention span. Friday morning is a good time to run such an event as it gives delegates an excuse to 'call it a week' at lunchtime. Offer a nice buffet lunch as a closer and a free afternoon demonstration of your product at work. Anyone who stays behind for this is a serious potential customer.

Afterwards, collate all information gathered. Not just names and email addresses but details about their company and their stories. Were there any buying signals? Now is the time to follow these up.

These targeted client seminars are the most effective account development tool I know – the equivalent to 100 sales visits in one day.

Sapling finance

When you can afford to make your part-time FD full time, do so. Then, as I've said before, listen to them. Maybe that's all I need to say, but here are some thoughts.

The basic principle of finance remains the same at sapling as at seedling level. Watch the cash.

The biggest difference is probably that cash can look more available to the sapling than it actually is. In the seedling, the cornerstones and even the entrepreneur usually have daily reminders that (to borrow a recent political slogan) there is no magic money tree. However, in the sapling, the business is ticking along and money is coming in regularly. Maybe such a tree has sprouted in that tiny little patch of ground behind the office after all.

It hasn't.

At the same time, of course, beware false economies such as outmoded technology or unmotivated but cheap call-centre staff intoning scripts. There is always a fine line to be drawn. The best way to draw it is to make the people spending the money have to convince a sceptical financial cornerstone that the expenditure really is necessary. If they make a good enough case, a purchase order is signed. If they don't make out a good enough case, they get a reasonable explanation.

One area where economies are almost always false is pay. However exciting and worthwhile your product, and even however fun your culture, bright, motivated people will not come and work for you for peanuts. Pay a little over the going rate, then monitor their progress carefully to make sure they are delivering value for that money.

Growing sapling businesses find themselves having to climb what we called in *Finance on a Beermat* ('we' being Chris, Stephen King and Jeff Macklin) the fixed cost staircase. In a perfect world, fixed costs, the ones we're stuck with whether we make any sales or not, would rise in a gentle upward curve as sales increased.

They don't, of course. Manufacturers can slowly use their existing machines more and more until they hit capacity, when they have to go out and get extra equipment. Maybe they have to get extra space to put it in too. Every time you take on a new person you add a new chunk of fixed cost to the business. The same is true if you open a new branch or a new office.

The team must work together planning for these sudden step rises in fixed costs.

Sapling funding

Just as at the seedling stage, avoid external finance if you can. Keep the orders flowing. Keep the customers paying on time. Keep outgoings as low as possible.

Use the bank as little as possible (which still may be quite a lot). Use secured loans for new assets. Have your finance cornerstone keep the bank regularly informed of how things are going. Banks hate surprises.

However, other sources of finance are available to the sapling enterprise. These may seem more exciting. In the end, banks make money from taking a margin on the money they lend you. They would like you to grow, but in the end they are more concerned that you don't go bust.

There are other, more daring sources of funding, whose main desire is that you grow and grow and grow. However, surprise, surprise – their support can come at a price.

The two main sources of 'investing for capital growth' funding are business angels and venture capitalists.

Business angels

Business angels are individuals with typically up to £1 million to invest in enterprises that attract them.

Angels fall into two categories. The first bring a huge amount to the party as well as money. They are mentors, with all those mentor benefits of experience and contacts. The best ones have fantastic market knowledge and have probably walked the course you are just starting on. Such people – I call them 'guardian angels' – can be amazing allies to a business.

Many such angels are former entrepreneurs who have made money and want to relive the experience again. They are not going to throw money away, but in the end they are on board for the ride. They will invest on gut feeling. Sure, you need a decent business plan to present to them, but in the end it's about personal chemistry. If the angel gets the entrepreneur, and to a lesser extent the top team, then they are more likely to climb on board.

Make it fun for them. Let them involve themselves in the business.

But at the same time, make sure they don't seize the controls. 'Investor relations' is a grand sounding term for the tricky business of managing the expectations of enthusiastic guardian angels. The entrepreneur is usually the best person to do this, but everyone has a part to play.

Much less attractive are what I call 'fallen angels' – investors who don't offer much mentoring but are just in it for the money. While you can't blame them, they are not the sort of people you want having influence over a sapling business, which is all about passion, products and people.

Where do you find the best type of angel? Most entrepreneurs are keen networkers and may well meet them in the course of this activity. Your mentor should be able to suggest some (they may even invest themselves, as I said earlier). Your finance cornerstone should also have their ear to the ground, especially checking out local angel networks. Local is important. Angels, especially those who want to get involved, prefer to invest locally.

Venture capitalists

Venture capitalists (VCs) are strictly only for start-ups that have enormous start-up costs and no conceivable way of bringing in any revenue till late in the development process. Traditionally they would only look at investments of above £5 million, though recently specialist 'early stage' VCs have started looking to put in amounts down to £1 million.

If you do fall into that tiny category of businesses that can only be funded by VCs, please be very careful in your dealings with these people. They have alluringly deep pockets, but are very ruthless. Get someone, or several people including accountants and lawyers, who are equally ruthless, on your side.

VCs can play games like stringing out negotiations, so the cash-hungry entrepreneur gets ever more desperate, then changing terms at the last minute. They can insist on fearsome clauses that virtually wipe out earlier investors. They have a reputation for promising more than they deliver in non-financial areas. They say they'll provide help with marketing and contacts, but in my experience they lose interest once the deal is signed. VCs tend to impose a fast growth model on any business in which they get involved. It's known as 'pumping and dumping', which nicely sums up what it feels like. If your plan is for anything other than hell-for-leather growth, you should find other sources of funding.

You've probably gathered I'm not a huge fan of VCs. I think they are far too interested in quick money and far too uninterested in what business is really about: people, creativity, commitment, adventure, delighted customers. However, I accept that in many cases they have helped businesses grow, especially in areas where massive start-up costs are hard to avoid and where there is a high level of risk.

I also accept that not all entrepreneurs are saints. A Ferrari can suddenly appear outside the company office after a round of funding that was supposed to help the business, not its owner. And not every VC fits the Dickensian stereotype I have presented. But I have met too many entrepreneurs who rue the day they took VC funding (to which the VC will no doubt reply that the entrepreneur didn't have to take it). I wish this were not the case, but that is my experience.

What all these 'big beast' investors, from the most helpful guardian angel to the worst kind of VC, have in common is that they want a slice of your equity for their money, and will want to cash this stake in at some time. There will be pressure for the company to be sold within a reasonably short time-frame. For many entrepreneurs and top teams, this is no problem. They want to cash in too. But if you have a different vision of a durable privately owned business which supports you and the team over many years, and which provides interesting work, stimulating workmates who become friends, and a civilized lifestyle, then be very cautious about this kind of investment.

An interesting alternative to angel or VC funding comes from Rupert Lee-Browne of Caxton FX, a company that facilitates foreign exchange transactions. Alert to the danger of watering down equity, he has gone through two rounds of financing by issuing bonds, repayable in five years' time and paying a healthy rate of interest over those years. Bonds are normally thought of as things that big companies issue, but Rupert did the classic entrepreneur thing and thought 'why not?' The bonds were largely bought by Caxton customers, who knew, liked and trusted the company.

The law

Sapling life is pretty similar to seedling here, except there's more going on.

Don't take on specialist legal staff. Keep legal expenditure down by using standard contracts. Talk to your customers. If you sense dissatisfaction brewing, address the issue quickly. Above all, stay away from the courts.

Now you have more contracts to watch, there is more opportunity for things to go wrong, so be alert.

Keep your employment contracts simple. Get the best from your HR consultant. And remember that, while contracts are necessary, the most important part of an employment agreement is unwritten and psychological. You're recruiting members of a tribe, and legal niceties are largely irrelevant to this.

High-technology saplings will continue to need the top-class patent lawyer they took on as seedlings.

Marketing

Different types of sapling need different levels of marketing. We never did much formal marketing at the sapling Instruction Set. We were a business services company. Consumer brands like Oppo Ice Cream are driven by it.

A tried and tested way of analysing marketing is the 4Ps: product, price, promotion and place.

Product

By products, remember, I don't just mean items but 'a definable set of benefits that someone can buy', i.e. a thing or a service or a combination of both.

Develop a range of these. Too big a range, unless you offer highly tailored ones, can create customer confusion. Too small a range, and you're missing out. A simple product range has three items in it – a taster, an old faithful ('Oh, yes, we sell a lot of those') and a premium product. A fourth, hyper-premium product can make the premium one look good value – and you never know, people might go for it.

At The Instruction Set we made our regular money from a standard 'Introduction to UNIX' course, our old faithful, and provided various premium, more specialist products to customers who wanted deeper technical knowledge.

Resist the temptation to tinker too much with an old faithful. Let it evolve slowly. Entrepreneurs and technical people often want to tinker endlessly with products. Salespeople can want to over-tailor them to the needs of their favourite customer. By contrast, finance people may want them not to change at all. Somewhere in between is the ideal.

Another 'P', packaging, comes under Product in the 4Ps model. For service businesses, this is not that important, though *Finance on a Beermat* co-author Stephen King tells the story of a cleaning company he advised, to whom he suggested they get uniforms for their staff. Initially the company resisted, then they trialled the uniforms, found that customers liked them, and were able to raise their prices.

However, when selling goods, especially through retail outlets, appearance matters greatly. Sales of Broker's Gin rose sharply after giving their bottle a makeover. In true entrepreneur style, Martin Dawson had the design done by a friend who was a professional designer, for 'mates rates'.

Price

A sapling company will know the value of what it offers the world, and charge accordingly.

I talk more about undercutting and price wars in the Help! section below.

Promotion

This doesn't just cover special promos but the general business of making the public aware of who you are and what you offer. Beermat promotion is about generating buzz, word of mouth, enthusiasm. Big consumer-product companies spend fortunes on trying to do this. Saplings can't afford to, so have to be imaginative.

Maybe you can guess I'm going to say this, but for service companies the best promotion is sales. A farmer conscientiously working an existing account, a hunter knocking on the doors of new ones. These need to be backed up by simple but excellent materials. Use PR if you like the idea. We never did, but I've seen other people work wonders with it. None should cost much.

Place

Where and how do people actually buy? Again, for many Beermat companies the answer is via a trusted salesperson. Other routes to market invite confusion and conflict of interest, though I accept that they are necessary for some businesses.

Remember the old marketing maxim: 'Make it easy for the customer to buy'. This sounds obvious, until you try buying online from a company that insists you set up an account, create a password, then asks you to follow instructions that don't make sense or to click on a link that doesn't work, all in order to buy a trowel for £1.99. Contrast this with Amazon's 'one click'.

Positioning

A fifth 'P' is positioning, which arguably comes before any of the above. It is the long-term consideration of strategy. Where do we sit in the market? Who are our rivals and how do we take them on? Who are our ideal customers? You started doing this when you asked 'Who will buy this?' that first night in the pub. You kept on doing it when you made a market map for your real business plan. Now you should be experts, knowing your key markets inside-out: who they are, what their pain is, how they like to buy.

I once suggested an idea to Jason Porter, co-founder of Friends Reunited. He pondered it, then shook his head and said, 'Our people wouldn't go for that.' To me, that is sapling strategic marketing.

When the company grows beyond the sapling stage, when they have decided that they want to (or in some cases, have to) take a whole market by the scruff of the neck and conquer it, then more complex strategic thought may be in order.

Social media

Much promotion now takes place via social media, so I have given this its own section. In it, I shall make some general points.

How intensely you use these media depends on the age of the people you are trying to reach. Millennials not only use social media but are greatly influenced by them. If you are selling to this age group, you need a social media strategy. How do you want the world to see you? How are you going to make sure they do that? Older customers use social media but are more sceptical about it.

If you have a social media wizard among your team, then use that expertise. If you haven't and you are selling to millennials, find an adviser.

This person's job will be to look after the technical side of social media – which ones you use, how often, what types of input work best. You must control the voice – the tone, the character. 'The modern trend is towards authenticity,' says social media consultant Kitty Underhill. 'Don't be corporate or advertisey – be yourself.' People have got tired of material from bots or people who sound like bots. Seedlings and saplings have particular advantages here as there is no pressure to be corporate.

However, there is a danger of going too far the other way. Authentic can easily morph into unguarded. Magnets long to be on Twitter, at the heart of every discussion, but they aren't always thoughtful about what they tweet. Your brand could be 280 characters away from serious damage. Have one of the top team be in charge of the content of your social media output, someone who can be chatty and authentic but stay grounded. The entrepreneur will want to be this person, but they may not be the right one. The foil might well be a better choice.

The social media scene is perpetually evolving. Right now, the ones below are the major ones – but no doubt this list will soon date. Especially if you are selling to millennials, you need to keep up with the changes.

LinkedIn

This is probably the most important medium for business. Get your profile right. Introduce yourself briefly, then say what problem you solve. Think back to the company's elevator pitch. If I am going on a sales visit, I always look at the LinkedIn profile of the person I'm about to see and note any areas of common interest.

Be cautious about who you let join your LinkedIn network. Not because they will do active harm, but because they will clog it up with attempts to sell you stuff or with news that you don't really care about. As I've said, the ideal network consists of about 150 people (more on this magic number in Chapter 4: The mighty oak). Make sure that this is the 150 you best know, like and trust. Keep in regular contact with them – and don't sell to them.

YouTube

This is another powerful medium. Small videos showing people how to solve simple problems in your field of excellence or do cool things with your product can build your reputation for expertise, and don't cost much to make. Keep them short, clear and to the point. Don't fret about production values, as long as the basics are covered: good sound, everything in focus. Many of the most popular YouTube videos are shot on phones.

Instagram

This is helpful for consumer products, especially foods. People will share pictures of your product, if you go overboard to make it look tasty. The next best thing to eating it, I guess.

Twitter

I've already mentioned Twitter and its potential for damage. Yet it is a useful tool. I use it most for research. What are people saying about my area of expertise? What are people saying about my business in particular?

If anyone's saying something nasty about you, you need to make a judgement. If you think they are a troll – there are plenty of these sad individuals – there's not much you can do. Counter any false statements, but otherwise ignore them. If you think the person is a reasonable individual who has either misunderstood something or caught you on a bad day, get on the case fast, promise to look into any complaints and keep your promise.

'Buzz' can be also generated on Twitter, but this is not the quick win it may seem to be. You need to have built a following first, which takes time and effort. Buzz is usually about a specific event, such as a sales seminar or product launch.

Facebook

Facebook is for me a strictly social thing for family and friends. It is saying that its latest algorithm (in 2018) is designed to keep it this way. However, at the same time it advertises its services to business. It seems to be nudging business users towards paying to boost their posts, thus removing one of the former advantages of social media, which is that they were free to use.

Facebook also offers the opportunity for more traditional pay per click advertising. If you are in a competitive area, the obvious search terms can be costly – and all you get for your money is a click. If you do go down this route, keep tight controls on budgets. Get a pro to write the ads and, even more important, the landing page, then test and measure, test and measure, test and measure.

Google

Google also offers pay per click advertising. The principles outlined in the paragraph above apply here, too.

Google ads or Facebook ones? Given the fast-changing nature of this sector, the best answer I can give is 'ask your expert adviser'.

Your website can also be a social medium if you post blogs and chat with people who comment on them.

Social media can be powerful, but can also gobble up time, attention and money. Worse still perhaps, these media can reward, and thus fuel, vanity. You're number one ranked for such-and-such a keyword, and have 1,500 followers on Twitter, and had 50 people like your last post (which didn't cost that much to boost, and was so worth it, as now all those wonderful people like you!). Great, but how much extra business has this brought in? Social media can make makers and monitors lazy, too, encouraging them to stay on their computers doing more tweeting and blogging, instead of doing the harder (for them) but more important stuff of getting out there and meeting people.

For the vast majority of substantial purchases, people still buy from people, real people they actually meet and then get to know, like and trust over time. For the Beermat business, the job of social media is to help that process, not replace it.

PR

Business-to-business companies get free PR by providing well-chosen news media with real news. Find out who the journalists are who cover your sector, especially in the specialist media, and get to know them. If your market is local, check out the local press, who can be very helpful. Look out too for freelancers who specialise in your sector.

If you have a well-known customer who is happy with your work, see if their PR department will work with you on a case study. These are the stories that the specialist publications really want – not dull product releases, but genuine customer stories of common problems neatly solved (by you, of course).

When you have a story, pitch it personally to your contacts. Sadly, most general press releases emailed or posted to publications go straight into the recycle or waste paper bin.

If you are selling to consumers, then you will want the attention of national media. They are much more difficult to deal with, and you can waste a lot of time trying to interest them. Off-the-scale magnet entrepreneurs may want to become media stars and will put their energies into that. A few manage this – well done, them – but remember that the media can turn against people very quickly. Actors, rock stars, artists and even politicians can get away with a certain amount of negative publicity. Businesses, especially Beermat ones, which are based on trust, can't.

However national media can deliver huge wins. The fledgling Friends Reunited was Steve Wright's Website of the Day on Radio 2 and had so many requests that the system crashed. Steve and Angela Sampson from

Paradise Wildlife Park appeared on Big Breakfast with Chris Evans – and Fred the Fox. Later they brought other animals on to the show, all of which charmed the public.

What about bad PR? Growing businesses are normally beneath the radar for this, unless they act deeply unethically, which, as a Beermat business, you won't. If for some reason you do get a negative spotlight turned on you, have the entrepreneur apologise for any mistakes, sort them out, then move on as quickly as possible.

Some businesses, for example, those offering services or experiences to the public like restaurants, retailers – or zoos – benefit greatly from PR. Other types of business need it less. We didn't use PR much at The Instruction Set.

If you fall into the latter category, don't be drawn into worrying about PR. Keep talking to your customers and execute superbly. Avoid public goofs by controlling your social media output. Act ethically. Grab positive PR opportunities when you can.

If you are in the former category, the kind that needs PR, do PR yourself if you have a knack for it. If you're a natural, you'll enjoy it. Don't become obsessed with it, however. Remember that the best PR only gets people through the door, after which you have to delight them. If self-promotion fills you with horror, find an adviser whom you know, like and trust.

Help!

However spot-on your vision and however masterly your execution, something will go wrong for the business at some time. Probably several things will go wrong at several times, and every now and then several things will go wrong at once.

Problems in sapling organisations nearly all come from quite simple sources. Here are some scenarios, and what to do if they arise.

- **You run out of cash**: Get selling, fast. I have more than once been told, 'If you don't sell something tomorrow, we're going broke.'

It certainly concentrates the mind. However, it shouldn't really happen. The finance cornerstone should be watching cashflow like a hawk. They should have an imaginary timetable of how many weeks till the closing down party, and when that total gets low, everyone should be put on red alert.

- **Costs out of control**: That's the other thing the finance cornerstone should be fixated with. Get pruning fast.

- **The bank withdraws the overdraft facility**: Talk. To your suppliers and customers about temporarily adjusting payment terms. To the bank about the possibility of a loan to cover the new cash hole. To other banks, whose managers may have 'new account' targets to meet. To everyone in the business, ensuring they understand the full gravity of the situation. To your mentor. To your life partner, as they must understand this is a highly stressful time for you. Sell assets. If you employ people, some may have to go. Stay strong.

- **Too many products**: This can happen if you over-customise, making sales unprofitable. Yes, very early on you should customise in order to find out what offers different types of customer want. Once you have established a typology of customers and created a range of products to suit them, stick to this range and evolve. The sales cornerstone, ever eager to give each customer exactly what they want, may not like this.

- **Downturn in the market**: A popular excuse for failure, but a bad one. Great companies survive the inevitable ups and downs of markets, and you are building a great company. The obvious answer to this problem is to work harder and smarter. But also consider that market downturns can be opportunities. Are some of your less fit competitors going to vanish? Supplies – and more important, quality people – will be cheaper.

- **Rival produces a better product**: Make an even better one. You have some leeway as your customers won't change at once. They like you. What they want to hear from you is, 'Yes, that is a great new product. But we're going to beat it – just watch.' It's also true that amazing new products can develop glitches. Don't panic, just put your innovation team on overdrive.

- **Rival produces an order of magnitude better product**: An example is what happened to Hoover when Dyson's cleaner came out.

This is a really tough one. Be very nice to your customers, to buy time. Get innovating fast. Look for disadvantages to the super new product. Few innovations are so perfect that there isn't some loss in changing from the old one to the new. If you find such a loss, play on your remaining advantage. Don't indulge in dirty tricks, both because you should have better ethics than that and because when the truth comes out people will despise you for it. Ideally, of course, you'd have your finger on the pulse of the industry so you can see these innovations coming.

- **A rival starts a price war**: Is there any way you could add extra service to what you do? Can you improve the spec of the product quickly? The key is to create clear water between yourself and the cheap rival. At the same time, try to find out if your rival has a real cost advantage. Is it something you can match? Or are they cutting corners in ways you think wrong in some way? I make an exception to my 'don't diss the opposition' maxim here. Don't do it in sales meetings, but if you think your adversary's approach is flawed, there are subtle ways of making the world aware of that. Not nice, but someone has just declared war on you. At the same time, don't start spreading false rumours.

  In most markets, buying market share is a short-term strategy that often rebounds on the price-cutter. Business customers know what the outcome will be – a near-monopolist who will suddenly turn round and ramp prices back up – and are distrustful of this kind of ploy. But they need reassurance from you. Talk to your customers and remind them of why your offer still represents good value for money. At the same time, expect them to trial the new, cheap product. Your customer mentors will tell you what they think of it. Your product should be better, so should see off the opposition. Of course, if you have a product that's worse and more expensive to produce, you deserve to be in trouble. Time to up your game.

- **Irregular flow of orders**: This is a problem often faced by small businesses. A big order comes in, all hands are put to the pump, maybe you take on extra hands, the order is delivered . . . then all goes quiet. This is the 'feast or famine' phenomenon. It is essentially a sales management problem. The sales cornerstone should have a systematic sales funnel and be moving potential customers through that all the time. Offer discounts at 'famine' times.

- **Overtrading**: Orders flow in, but cause delivery or cashflow problems. As a salesperson, it breaks my heart to hear about this. If the marketplace is biting your arm off for your product, this is a huge win. So many great-sounding products don't sell, so an unexpected level of customer demand has to be fantastic news. But it clearly does create difficulties elsewhere in the organisation. I'm afraid this means late nights at the office for the delivery and finance cornerstones, and the entrepreneur too.

  Get networking, get thinking fast on who you could team up with to get the delivery issues sorted. When you get a new and workable delivery plan in place, your bank – with whom you have a good relationship because your finance cornerstone keeps them up to date with your financial state – should be prepared to lend to you on the basis of a bulging order book and that plan. Incidentally, it's worth examining your internal communication if the overtrading problem arises. Didn't the sales cornerstone have clear targets, agreed by the board and in line with the real business plan? The moment sales began to exceed targets, why weren't the rest of the top team informed? Yes, orders can suddenly flood in, for example, after an unexpected piece of publicity, but a much more common scenario is that the problem is allowed to build gradually because parts of the business have stopped talking to one another.

- **A supplier suddenly lets you down**: Obviously, try to negotiate some kind of delivery from them. But assume the worst. Don't waste time being angry, although you've a right to be. You have more important things to do. Work with the sales and delivery cornerstones to schedule what you can still deliver and what orders you will have to delay. Talk to the latter group of customers at once and explain what has happened. If your sales cornerstone has been doing their job properly, your customers will like you and be understanding – for a while. This gives you a window of opportunity to source new supplies. Get networking. Talk to all your contacts, including your customers, to find out as much information about alternatives as possible. Talk to your mentor and set them networking too. Of course, the best remedy for this is to have alternative suppliers on hand. Just as your sales cornerstone has a list of prospects, your delivery cornerstone should have a list of prospective suppliers. If possible, you should be sourcing some stuff from them already.

- **A big customer deserts you**: This is perhaps the biggest nightmare of all. I talked about this in the section on sales above. Try and get a termination clause written into the initial contract – and have a Plan B waiting in the wings. Put this plan into action at once, and start working on Plans C, D and E.

In all emergencies . . .

- Accept there is a problem and go into overdrive . . .
- . . . but don't panic.
- Get the top team together to work on this.
- Talk to everyone else in the company, including your mentor, any non-execs and trusted advisers (where relevant).
- Gather as much information as possible as quickly as possible.
- Leave the emotions (anger, blame, guilt, etc) for later.
- Once you have decided on the way forward, act quickly and decisively.

Remember that all enterprises encounter unforeseen difficulties. Someone once described them as 'elephant traps' – one moment you're walking happily along, the next you're at the bottom of a large hole. It is moments like this when entrepreneurs, and foils and cornerstones, but especially entrepreneurs, show their steel and do whatever it takes to save the business they love.

Great businesses get out of traps. They benefit from the experience. The team is stronger. Useful lessons are learnt about how to deal with certain problems – and, often, about who your friends really are. The episode becomes part of the company culture: 'Do you remember that time when . . . ?'

OK, occasionally they don't get out. It might, just might be the case that the elephant trap is inescapable. If you challenge an established big brand, they may simply declare unrelenting, total war on you. Coke and

Pepsi crushed Virgin Cola. However, Adam Balon, one of the team behind the ill-fated cola, learnt from the experience and co-founded his own business in an adjacent but less 'owned' market, the hugely successful Innocent Smoothies, which, ironically, ended up being bought by Coke.

Entrepreneurs don't give up, though they may be forced after much resistance to make a tactical retreat. Think very deeply about what went wrong, then come back, stronger and wiser. My view is that when you do come back, it's best to emulate Adam Balon and stick to your general area of expertise – in his case, the retailing of drinks – but to approach it from a fresh angle. That is where you have experience, knowledge and contacts, and where the harsh lessons you have just learnt should prove most relevant.

The big decision – boutique or big one?

As I've said, you can function as a sapling for a long time. 25 people, really committed to the vision and its realisation. Happy customers. A reputation for excellence. It's a fantastic way to be in business. 'We're 25 people and we like it that way,' says Juliet Price of her business, Park City Consulting.

Your business might look like this . . .

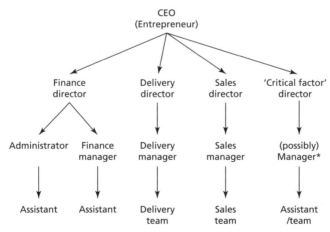

* The Critical Factor director might manage a small team directly

As your reputation builds, flattering things start happening:

- You start getting CVs sent to you. The recruitment industry has spotted you and knows that you hire people from time to time. Sadly, most of these CVs will be irrelevant. Stick to your traditional, more personal way of recruiting.

- Bright individuals may well contact you personally. Treat this as a compliment. Send a polite reply and keep these approaches on file. If your informal, network-based recruiting system stutters for some reason, dig these out and see if any fit the bill.

- Bankers and VCs start contacting you, offering loans, money for equity stakes, etc. Treat this as a threat, like that charming person at the bar selling drugs. The finance cornerstone knows what the business needs and has the contacts to ensure the business gets it. A strict financial discipline can be overturned by a sudden rush of easy money, especially when it turns out not to be as easy as you thought, due to some interesting anti-dilution clauses buried deep in the deal.

  A particularly scary approach runs along these lines. 'X [one of your cornerstones] hasn't been performing well recently, has he?' (No, but how the hell did this creep find that out?) 'If you had some of all this cash I've got, you could buy him out – and let *me* come on board instead. I have lots of contacts that could be really helpful for you. How much was X's stake? 25%. I'd be happy with that.'

- The press ring up for comment on developments in your area. Great news! Be as helpful as you can. Rupert Lee-Browne got a call from a journalist and spent time talking him through what was then a new, disruptive business. Rupert even suggested names of competitors the journalist should speak to. Shortly afterwards, a piece appeared on the back of the *Sunday Telegraph*, complete with a quote describing Caxton FX as 'a little goldmine'.

- You get a sudden rush of interest from abroad. 'We've heard about your amazing company, product or service. We'd like to buy some of your product, or to represent you in x-land (where x-land is a fashionable and currently booming market). Can we visit you?' Beware! Assume this is a competitor trying to find out more about you. I've seen breathtakingly cheeky industrial espionage carried out by pretend customers. One of my first jobs was at an experimental plant making cleaning products from sugar. A 'potential customer' from overseas sent a team 'just to see how the technology works', and spent hours photographing the equipment and asking deep technical questions. At the time, I was too junior to stop them. We never saw them again, of course.

- It could also be a PhD student – less of a threat, it might seem, but a waste of time and a potential source of IP leakage.
- Maybe the person is a wheeler-dealer who wants to act as an intermediary. Even if they are sincere, they are unlikely to add much value. If you want to crack an overseas market, research it, and either go in yourself, slowly and respectfully, or select the right partner.

The key in all the above cases is to qualify, qualify, qualify. Do the people getting in touch have needs and money today? If their company does turn out to be reputable, make them pay for a timed, exclusive, non-refundable option.

It is time to start asking yourself if you should consider further growth.

If your company grows further, its nature will change radically – whether you want it to or not. It's to do with the psychology of how many people one can really know well and trust.

Beyond around 25 people, the organisation of the business has to become more bureaucratic. The way you hire staff changes. The kind of people you hire changes. You may find yourself needing bigger premises: another culture change. You may split premises and have offices in two places, which changes the culture even more. The kinds of business done by the company seem to change as well. You need bigger income flows – and can get them. But in getting these, you are probably emerging out of your niche and flexing your muscles to take on all-comers. The big players start noticing you, and they don't usually hang out a sign with 'Welcome' on it. Once you have left your niche, it is almost impossible to scuttle back.

If you grow beyond the sapling stage, you must do so as the result of a *positive decision*. You must accept you are entering a new phase in the life of the business, and plan accordingly.

I have worked with start-ups that drifted beyond saplinghood into a kind of limbo, where they still wanted to operate and feel like a sapling, but just couldn't. Old hands started complaining. 'The company isn't like it used to be' and 'Nobody listens to me any longer'. Newcomers didn't know who everybody was. Last week, the entrepreneur bumped into someone in the corridor and didn't have a clue who they were. These businesses didn't last long in this state. Either they grasped the nettle and went for growth, with all its accompanying costs, or they fell apart.

Moving on can be a painful experience. Big companies are less fun than small ones. There'll be more stress. Ironically, people feel lonelier in them.

If you go for growth, you should end up with a substantial financial reward. You will work incredibly hard in an environment that is not really your natural one, but hopefully not for more than four or five years, at the end of which you will not need to work again.

It will be one hell of a challenge. Can you really turn it down?

Most entrepreneurs will have no doubt. They love their business and want to see it as successful as possible.

Cornerstones should be more thoughtful. There are five key criteria by which to judge their suitability to grow:

- **The market**: You must believe you have the ability to conquer a big marketplace. By conquer, I don't mean monopolise but become a market leader (or at least challenge for that role).
- **Sales**: You must have a regular flow of sales, from a decent range of customers. Sometimes your customers actually ask you to grow. Sometimes they beg you to. If they really like the service they get from you, they will want more of it than a mere sapling can provide. In this case, you have very little choice, as if you don't offer them your product on the scale they have started to require,

they will be forced to go elsewhere and find someone who provides something not quite as good but in the quantities they need it.

- **Organisation**: You should have an efficient, established infrastructure with day-to-day tasks like payroll, delivery and security under control.
- **Finance**: You should have a healthy credit rating. How much can you borrow?
- **People**: This is probably the most important criterion of all. Everyone in the business must be crystal-clear about how they feel about making the change.

Time to move on?

- Market belief
- Sales flow and variety
- Sound organisation
- Solid finances
- People in agreement and prepared

The best way to ensure a successful transition from sapling to growing oak is to confront the team with the decision a long time before it happens – when your staff level gets to 14 or 15. 'Some time in the future, we'll be faced with this choice. What do you think about it?' That way, when the crunch time comes, they'll be clear about which way they want to jump. And that's what you need: 25 clear decisions.

My experience is that most people will see the challenge and the prospective financial rewards – and the dangers of trying to stay small if you are in a fast-expanding market – and jump at the chance. Those who are unwilling will probably have to leave, unless some new, off-centre role can be found for them.

Those who are up for the change must brace themselves for a change in work style, as the place becomes colder and more bureaucratic.

When you decide to change, draw up a new business plan. This plan, which I call your 'Market Conquest Plan', looks like the fantasy business plans that blossomed back in the dotcom era. Only it's about a real business with a real track record and realistic ambitions. The sales are real, the markets are real. You actually expect to meet the targets. Maybe you'll even exceed them.

Drawing up a Market Conquest Plan is the ideal way to end your time as a sapling. As you do so, you must know in your bones that the plan is going to work, that it is a road map and not a dream. You really do understand the market, you really do know your potential customers.

The tribe is about to move off the savannah into the first towns.

Life will never be the same again.

The mighty oak

The change when you get beyond 25 people (or thereabouts) is dramatic. Formal procedures have to be introduced. New people are employed who don't have quite the same spark, commitment or eccentricity of the dream team. And someone puts a lock on the stationery cupboard.

If you have enjoyed this book so far, you may not believe you are cut out for life in this new phase of the story. All those forms and procedures are what you joined a start-up to get away from.

Your belief may not be right. Some people make the transition. They are sharp enough to see the change coming and treat it as a whole new adventure. 'Right, now I'm going to learn how to do things the corporate way!' Your sapling managers may well fall into this category. For them, their experiment with working in a sapling will turn out to have been a stepping stone to more conventional, senior positions.

However, in essence my advice to top teams who have decided to grow from sapling to mighty oak is 'start hiring grown-ups'. By this, I mean industry-specialist managers who are experienced in running departments, keeping projects on budget and on time, and (above all) managing people. Then, of course, let these individuals manage. Don't meddle, don't 'get a dog and bark yourself'.

Learn from them too.

In the modern gig economy, good people can be brought in on consultancy contracts. If they gel, they may stick around.

The mighty oak stage will be a time of reflection for entrepreneur, cornerstones and dream team alike. Before, they all knew what they were in business for. They did it for love, for the buzz, for the challenge, for the tribal adventure (and money too of course). But now things are changing. Now money looms ever larger. Salaries are bigger, as are expense accounts, and for entrepreneur and cornerstones a giant payout is appearing on the horizon if they decide to go down particular exit routes. But it's not as much fun.

People and culture

One thing remains constant, at least – business is still essentially about people. But just as your dream team players were different from your fellow founders, you will be recruiting different sorts of individuals into the growing oak: *employees.*

Employees are unlikely to feel the same level of loyalty to the company as dream-teamers. Instead, they are specialists – good ones – selling you their skills at the market rate. So buy those skills, treat the vendors fairly and don't expect the kind of commitment you got from the dream team.

Don't totally give up on the culture, however.

Keep looking for cultural fit as you take people on. Keep looking for SWANs and keep out energy sappers, even if they have the perfect qualifications for the job.

We still had our Instruction Set team gatherings once we got beyond 25 people, with awards and rounds of drinks paid for by the company. And they were fun, but never quite as much fun as those sapling ones. We still felt loyalty to our people. Even employee number 150 was still special. But not quite as special as the original dream team.

We tried to keep the old 'mates' recruiting system going, but also ran a parallel process of advertising, sorting through applications, setting up interviews and so on. We kept introducing people we wanted to hire to as many people in the company as possible before actually taking them on, but that got harder and harder to do.

Here are some suggestions on how to keep the company as fresh and entrepreneurial as possible once you enter this new stage:

- Take time, resources and effort to recruit individuals with the right attitude. This is probably the single most important thing.
- If narcissistic, energy-sapping individuals sneak in through your recruitment system, have ways of getting them out as quickly and painlessly as possible – and review your hiring procedures so this doesn't happen again.

- If you can recruit slowly but regularly, do so. It's easier to 'enculturate' people one at a time or in small groups.
- Once the right people are on board, treat them like dream-teamers as much as possible (see Chapter 3: The sapling enterprise).
- Have a system for encouraging intrapreneurship and, more generally, positive suggestions. Act on the suggestions that come through this system, trialling them, unless you feel very strongly that they are unethical, expensive or won't work.
- Keep having group events (meals, days out, etc) paid for by the company.
- Encourage online groups. MiddletonMurray has three WhatsApp groups where employees share personal achievements, both at work and outside it. Founder Angela Middleton also uses the service to chat with employees.
- Make stock options part of everyone's reward.
- Know everyone's name. This gets ever harder as the company grows, but hugely worth the effort.
- Keep your office door as open to anyone in the business as much as possible (figuratively, as in the MiddletonMurray example above, but also literally). This becomes harder and harder as the business gets bigger and you get busier. Ian Walker of Laundry Republic sums it up neatly: 'Be approachable but not always available.'
- Show 'institutional' concern for the wellbeing of your team members. Progressive modern companies have gyms on site (if they have the space) and organise mindfulness and other personal development sessions. At the same time, allow people who are cynical about such things to be heard.
- Keep believing in the core values – and practising them. The business can be seen as a leaky tank into which you are pouring your spirit. If you stop doing this, the passion and belief will disappear incredibly quickly, and it will turn into a bureaucracy.

Some businesses manage to keep an intense company culture for a long time. That's a magnificent achievement.

Another magic number

150 employees may well be another milestone, though I think it is much less significant than 5 or 25. This is the Dunbar number, named after anthropologist Robin Dunbar, who argued that this was the maximum size for a community of people who can have a 'real social relationship' with one another. Dunbar worked this out from studies into the brain sizes of primates and correlating this with the size of groups they chose to live in. He then sought to corroborate his findings by looking at anthropology – what do people actually do? He found that people often formed what he called 'bands' of around 30 people, and beyond that groups of between 150 and 200.

He also found that in both sizes of group, people spent a lot of time doing what he called social grooming – chatting, doing stuff together. The term comes from chimps, who spend a huge amount of time actually grooming each other. No, I'm not going to advocate that we regularly stop work and start picking nits out of each other's hair (though no doubt it's only a matter of time before some hip management guru comes along and suggests exactly this). But it does show the importance of keeping the workplace human, even in the 150-person organisation.

Intriguingly, we sold The Instruction Set at almost exactly this point, 150 people, purely by chance rather than expertise in anthropology.

Cornerstone burnout

As I have said, some cornerstones and dream team players (and some entrepreneurs) don't feel at home in the mighty oak world. Or they do feel at home, so much so that they keep working at the rate they did in the first years of the company and begin to show signs of serious stress: cornerstone burnout.

If either of these is the case, they must be replaced, permanently.

This replacement is operational. Their place in the mythology of the company must remain intact. If a cornerstone wants or burns out, keep them as an unsalaried founder director. Insist they take a long, long-dreamt-of, holiday, or a year out to write that thriller they always talked about (you know, the one about a serial killer in a small software business). When they return, create a left-field corporate role for them.

If they want to cash in their stake, as at the sapling stage, you need to establish a fair valuation for the business. This is harder to do now, as there's more money involved, but it has to be done. As at the sapling stage, get your mentor involved.

If your finance cornerstone will let you fund the burnt-out cornerstone's exit from cash, that's the best way. If not, find an alternative – a staggered pay-out or a quick sale of some underused assets. Do all you can to avoid getting into debt or giving away equity to fund the pay-out.

Best of all, avoid this. I recommend mandatory two-week annual holidays for the entrepreneur and cornerstones. You now have managers to run the show on a day-to-day basis. So forget all the machismo about working 167 hours a week, 52 weeks a year, and even the metaphor about entrepreneurship being a marathon. Marathon runners don't stop for the odd five-minute break. Take time off. All of you.

During your 50 working weeks, look after yourself. Eat properly. Exercise. Entrepreneur Monique Drummond recommends practising mindfulness – there are a number of apps available with meditations you can listen to.

If a cornerstone does, despite doing the above, burn out, you have to find a good replacement. Your mentor is a great place to start. They are bound to know some quality people with experience of managing big businesses. Note how the mentor remains important in this phase of the life of the business. Mentoring isn't just about starting up. Top sports-people keep coaches long after they have achieved more than the coach ever did. They know that you never stop learning, and that part of learning is to have an excellent teacher.

If your mentor can't come up with anyone, try your own contacts.

The new people you take on into the mighty oak may also have contacts.

Headhunters are a last resort. If you do find yourself using this last resort, make sure they don't start acting unethically and stealing people from your rivals. I know this advice may sound goody-goody, but this kind of practice is quietly corrosive to your running of an ethical, effective business, and to the kind of morale and loyalty such a business uniquely commands. You might win a few points in the short term, but it is a loser's strategy over time.

Note that if someone tries to poach your staff, it's a signal that the opposition are getting a bit desperate. If it succeeds, it shows you're not managing well enough to keep key people loyal.

Killing the king

The most difficult person to replace is the entrepreneur, but if you go for growth it often has to be done at some time. Just as parents never really quite see their children as adults – especially when you bring a new partner to meet them and they start telling that story of the time you peed in the paddling pool aged four – in their heart, the entrepreneur is still king or queen of the dynamic seedling, waving their original beermat like a revolutionary manifesto and ready to conquer the world.

The kind of passionate, charismatic leadership that got the entrepreneur this far often isn't appropriate any longer, and the cracks can start to show. For example, they start building a praetorian guard, a clique of people loyal to them, not to the company, and these guards start doing things in direct contravention of company policy. Or the entrepreneur's public behaviour becomes bizarre towards customers or employees. Or they make unwise statements to the press or via social media.

We can all cite examples of model entrepreneurs who haven't done this, but I have seen it happen so often that you must be prepared for it. It's important not to be judgemental at this time. The entrepreneur is under huge stress. They are working incredibly hard, having to make decisions that impact ever more people. Harder still, they are seeing something they love morph into something different. They've lost their tribe. But if they are handling the stress dysfunctionally, they must be removed from operational responsibility or they can drag the business down.

It is of course the cornerstones' job to do this, and it is probably one of the hardest things they will ever do. By far the best way is for all four cornerstones to go off-site with the entrepreneur, and your mentor if possible, and *persuade* the entrepreneur that the best thing, for everyone's sake, would be for them to move on.

There is no simple way of doing this, but the following hints have proven useful:

- Be united. Agree in advance among the four of you what you want the outcomes of the discussion to be.
- Consider other areas of discussion where the entrepreneur can negotiate *and win.*
- Try to see things from the entrepreneur's point of view. Remember, they love the business like no one else does.
- Ask what their issues or their problems might be. How can moving on be presented to them as a solution to these issues and problems?
- Don't threaten them. That creates instant conflict and defensiveness. Yes, you have the boardroom power (or will have if you've built a Beermat company), but don't flaunt it.
- Don't just comment negatively. The more you can frame the discussion in a positive context – 'Look how far we've come in ten years' – the better. The 'but . . . ' that follows will still hurt, but it will do so less than a simple diet of rejection.
- Comment on specific behaviours, rather than making a blanket criticism of them as a person. The more the entrepreneur takes it personally, the more defensive they will become. Of course, they will take it personally, but your job is to *minimise* this reaction. You should know them well enough to know when they are going into hurt child mode. Have you expressed something badly? Stop the conversation at this point and remind them you are not having a hate session aimed at them, but just trying to solve a problem.
- Stay in control of yourself. You may want to let rip after what the entrepreneur has been up to recently, but now is not the time. If they start getting personal with you, don't go down that road. They're upset, remember. Whatever they say, don't hold it against them.

- The entrepreneur must save face. Have a golden escape route ready for them. ('Our CEO is moving on to concentrate on strategic issues as our new President.') Use your knowledge of them, and your imagination, to design a route which would really appeal to them.

These suggestions are not magic formulae, however. This won't be easy or fun. But this way is a lot less miserable than a simple show of board-room voting power and the inevitable backlash. Companies have been destroyed by former leaders who have been insensitively disposed of and who then seek revenge.

If you are the entrepreneur in this situation, please go gracefully, while at the same time negotiating the best possible outcome for yourself. Part of you will feel deeply hurt, but don't let that part take over and start a war with the rest of the team. You'll probably feel an overpowering temptation to do something really spiteful to those bastards who have turned round and stabbed you in the back and that ungrateful company that isn't your baby any longer. Resist it.

This is a deep personal loss. Such loss triggers a natural grief process, which is often characterised as denial, anger, bargaining and finally acceptance.

You can't follow that. You have to do the bargaining first, which can be difficult. Buy a little time to work through these phases as much as you can.

How do you express your anger normally? A Siouxsie and the Banshees tribute band? Whacking the hell out of a helpless golf ball? The written word? Go and see a therapist too. Rant and rave at them. Whatever you do, *don't* let your rage loose in your family home or in your workplace. But don't just lug it around with you, either.

Get your head as clear as possible, then negotiate.

Then once the negotiations are over, make a clean break, during which you treat yourself to something extravagant, something you've always wanted to do but never had time for.

Accept what you have achieved. You have changed the world. You have provided for yourself and your family a standard of living unimaginable to most people on the planet, and beyond the reach of 99% of your compatriots.

Most of all, perhaps, accept that this change was inevitable. Few entrepreneurs make the transition from start-up to corporate boardroom wholly successfully. There is no shame attached to having to go when the time is right. The complete opposite, in fact.

Remember the old adage that the best revenge is a happy life. Get yourself back in balance, enjoying life.

When it's time to go . . .

- Understand why: This is a common experience for successful entrepreneurs
- Handle your anger: Let it out in 'safe' ways
- Negotiate a good exit
- Make a clean break: Treat yourself to something fantastic
- Be proud of what you've done
- Remember: 'The best revenge is a happy life'

For the rest of the team, the money has to be found to buy the entrepreneur out. This will most likely be a bigger stake than any of the cornerstones', so even if you have been a model Beermat business and funded from revenue, you may well be unable to fund such a sizeable and sudden cash-call. Can the entrepreneur keep some of their shares, with the upside that those shares will be worth more in a few years' time?

You may have to deal with angels or VCs at this point. Move heaven and earth to find a guardian angel, and to steer clear of anyone who will trample all over the company culture and turn it into a ruthless exercise in pumping and dumping.

This is why part of the job of the finance cornerstone, even in a revenue-funded company, is to keep networking with funders, and to know which ones like the business and are right for it culturally, should they be needed.

Meanwhile, the entrepreneur has to be replaced. As with finding cornerstones, talk to the mentor first and use personal contacts if possible. This is the time to find a top industry professional, skilled in operating a big company. They will bring in new ideas. The company's learning process continues.

Non-execs

As well as cornerstones, you can have other sources of leadership at your disposal. Your mentor should be a non-executive chair of the business. And how about some other non-executive directors? We never had any at The Instruction Set, but I know other businesses that took one or two on and found them very useful once they decided to go for mighty oak growth.

Non-execs are people who aren't involved in running the business, but who sit on the board and bring to it expert knowledge.

Just as with cornerstones, recruit them personally. When you've done so, use them well. They have expertise and influence but can only use these if you are totally honest with them. It's no use treating them like a teacher or parent you want to hide things from (don't laugh – I've seen people do it). The more they know – warts and all – about the business, the more help they can be.

Non-execs can be of particular use if you have one specific problem that none of the founders or the mentor seem able to solve. Go and ask their help, and it's amazing what they can do.

Sadly, not all non-execs fall into the above category. There are two types of non-exec who are worse than useless.

One is the 'letterhead non-exec'. I have seen several companies where retired celebs or members of the aristocracy are made non-exec directors, in a bid to impress people with their name on the notepaper. This is silly. Nobody of any importance is impressed by this. Of course, if the celeb or aristo has genuinely useful contacts that they really can and do activate, then they can earn the privilege of being part of your fantastic, hard-built business. But often they don't.

The other is the externally appointed (i.e. imposed) non-exec, placed on boards by outside equity holders. My experience of these people has not been good. They spend board meetings quibbling about minutiae, raising irrelevant points and generally trying to show everyone how clever they are. Of course, if you've sold a chunk of your business to a capital provider, then you may well have to put up with this kind of bumptious show-off. This is another reason for funding from revenue or, if you must get money in from outside, taking the time and effort to find the right kind of angel.

Non-execs on a Beermat

- You respect them
- They respect you
- They have contacts and experience
- They bring a fresh perspective to the party
- They're nice to work with

Other aspects

Looking at the various other aspects of mighty oak business, rather than just trying to replicate what the management textbooks tell you, I will just make a few observations.

Funding

Once you reach that critical mass of around 150 people, and have substantial assets and a good track record, you are now in a position to talk to 'big money' if you want to. Their risk in providing capital for you is much less than it would have been at the start of things, so you can negotiate tough terms with them – terms that keep most of the equity where it belongs, in the hands of the people doing the work, whatever the outcome of things. We still recommend getting some extra-sharp people on your side if you do go down this route.

Or remember the Caxton FX story in the previous chapter and think about issuing bonds.

Law

I still don't think you should take on lawyers full time, because the basic principle of 'Don't litigate, negotiate' remains constant whatever the size of your company. But clearly the more business you do, the more legal issues are likely to arise. If you only used a small firm at the start, you may need to look for a bigger outfit to advise you, especially when you start doing business overseas (or when you start talking to VCs or thinking about selling). Have a stiff drink to hand when their first bill arrives.

Globalisation

Don't race into the global marketplace. It's tougher than it looks. Despite a veneer of similarity (McDonald's in Beijing, Kenyan kids in Nike baseball caps), the world's markets are all very different from one another. Growing companies can blunder into overseas markets, assuming that if they do it 'like they do at home plus a few tricks learnt off the locals', they'll crack it. Usually, this fails. Some very big companies that really should know better have made this mistake too. Please don't throw away all that hard work you've put in by opening 17 offices round the world simultaneously.

My tip on going international is 'let the market choose you'. If you suddenly start getting orders from Germany, have a go at the German market. If you secure one big client in an overseas market, set up a tiny office there to service that client, and quietly see what other business you can build up while you're there.

We went international in The Instruction Set, but only after a great deal of interest from the US. We chose our location to be on the doorstep of our biggest customer. Apart from two Brits – the sales cornerstone (me) and a sapling manager – in charge, we employed local people. The US subsidiary was a big success. It was included in the deal when we sold the company, but later did a management buy-out, and is still flourishing.

Stock options

Set up a system to share the wealth that your people are helping you create.

The UK has the excellent Enterprise Management Incentive (EMI) scheme whereby options on shares can be granted to employees, tax free for them and with no National Insurance charge for the company. The scheme also allows employees to buy shares in the company at a discount. The system is for businesses with up to 250 employees, though some businesses such as farming and property development are not allowed to participate. The maximum value of shares that can be issued in this way is £3 million. I shan't go into further detail about this as your finance cornerstone should know about it.

The scheme does need to be managed correctly, but that's what you have a finance cornerstone for.

It is a big regret of mine that we did not have a stock option system at The Instruction Set. My excuse is that it was much less common in those days. In the modern entrepreneurial workplace, such systems are common. Tony Waller reckons that your stock option scheme should represent about 10 to 15% of the business' equity.

The big decision: when to sell

Almost all entrepreneurs and cornerstones take their businesses into the mighty oak stage with an exit in mind. It keeps them going in what is essentially an alien environment. 'We'll put up with this big business stuff for three years, then we'll be big enough to get taken over or go public.'

But when, exactly, do you sell?

The obvious answer is 'When someone makes you a good enough offer.' But what is 'good enough'?

There are essentially two aspects to this decision. One is a reading of the market, the other is your reading of yourself.

There is usually a compelling *market* logic to a sale. Most exciting new markets begin fragmented, with lots of small players, then coalesce into more mature markets which have fewer but bigger players plus a few tiddlers surviving in highly specialist niches. It's hard to buck this trend. There are essentially four options for a 150-person company in a sector that is changing in this way:

- Grow to be a major player.
- Get swallowed up by a major player, often one in an adjacent sector that wants a slice of the new action.
- Lurk in a very specialist niche (you may already be too big for this, as it is often a sapling gig).
- Pretend this isn't happening, chunter along, see your customers poached as major players steam into the market, and go bust.

The 150-person Instruction Set found itself surrounded by some very big IT service companies that had suddenly realised they needed UNIX skills. They had two ways of getting these. One was by buying people like us; the other was by recruiting and training up their own specialists. It made sense for them to buy a 'box' of ready-made expertise (and contacts), ready for instant use. We were suddenly in demand. But only for a while. Right then, we brought our big suitors time. The longer we played the field, the less of this we offered. In the long run, they could have all set up their own UNIX-savvy departments and made us irrelevant.

It was a bit like life for a heroine in a Jane Austen novel, where she has a few bright years on the marriage market, during which she has to make the best of herself and find a partner, or risk turning into a spinster, which was not a great gig in Regency Britain. Miss Bates in *Emma*, for example: 'poor; she has sunk from the comforts she was born to; and if she live to old age, must probably sink more'. Don't become a Miss Bates business.

The *inner* problem can be a bigger one. Once your company grows, it's easy to become convinced that you are going to be the next Amazon, LinkedIn (or whatever). 'Look at the founders of those companies. They're not just worth millions but billions! And we could be like them!'

A serious dose of realism is needed. When I mentor entrepreneurs and this subject comes up, I get them to think through how much money they would actually like to have. The way to answer this question is to forget about money. Instead, think about what *real* things they would like. A bigger house? A decent pension pot? Money for the kids' education? An amazing car? A stunning holiday twice a year? Some cash to act as an angel and help other start-ups? The chance to fund a charity?

Once you have worked out your list, work backwards. How much would all these cost? The answer is not a hundred million pounds. So what's the point of risking the company – your wealth, the careers of your people, the culture you have created – in pursuit of 'monopoly money', fabulous but still only theoretical wealth?

Inner discipline is required to keep to this target. Remember the old investor's maxim: 'When selling, leave something in the stock for someone else.'

Dealing with offers

Offers will come your way. Some are less serious than others.

Some offers are tactics from rivals. They can be in pursuit of information about your company. Tell us your secret and we'll make an offer. Or they can be simply to hold you up, to waste your time and energy. They may be flirtations. 'Well, we might be interested . . . '

As with sales, offers, especially the most attractive ones (to keep the Jane Austen theme going, Mr Darcy, fresh from his dip in the lake), have to be given a sanity check early on. Create a heads of agreement as soon as possible. This should specify a price, and, just as important, a time limit after which the agreement is void (and the offer can be rejected as non-serious). A month is a sensible such limit. This time limit should be welcome to a serious suitor. They're buying you for the time you save them, so they want to get on with it too.

Once this is agreed, prepare for tough negotiations (though never forget this is ultimately about creating a win–win outcome). Be thorough. If there are deal-breakers in the contract, get them removed and be prepared to walk away if they are not.

You will encounter tactics of varying degrees of legitimacy. The one I like least is the last-minute change of mind. The deal is nearly ready, then suddenly the buyer announces that 'the market has changed' or that they've 'been thinking' (or some other excuse), and that the terms have to change – in their favour, of course. A particularly nauseating version of this is when the buyer initially encourages you to go round telling everyone about the nearly-done deal, then hits you with this sudden change.

Faced with this kind of trickery, you have to be tough, above all with yourself. In your mind, you are already sitting on the beach sipping a cocktail in A-list company. Snap out of it. You're sitting in an office drinking machine-made coffee in the company of some people who have just revealed themselves to be reptiles. You have to seize the initiative back. Tell the buyers that this is not acceptable and that they have an hour to revoke these new conditions or you are walking out. Walk out if they don't. Bye bye, beach – for now. The potential buyers may come running after you. If not, your consolation is that these people were not fit owners for your business anyway.

More subtle wheezes include pacing negotiations so that big demands come at the end of long sessions, often when you are hungry. It's amazing how hunger will overpower willpower and reason. 'OK, I agree to that! *Now* can we have some dinner . . . ' The key here is to know when you are getting hungry or tired and call a halt to proceedings. Start again refreshed.

When we sold The Instruction Set, the entrepreneur and the foil, who had set up the deal, also did most of the negotiating. I was called in 'just to sign things' at five in the afternoon. I was happy with this, as I trusted these two people totally (and still do). Even so, the negotiations got strung out, and we ended up all signing at two in the morning. Most big deals are signed at crazy hours.

So keeping fit, sleeping soundly and eating well are all part of negotiation.

After the sale, be prepared for *seller's remorse*. This may seem odd. Haven't you become rich? Yes. But someone will no doubt tell you that you could have got more from XYZ PLC. A rival may well sell for a better earnings multiple a few months later.

There is also genuine loss to be dealt with. The Instruction Set culture vanished the moment we sold out. We had already had to negotiate about our employees behind their backs. Openness had been a key part of our culture, but legally we had no choice but to conceal this potential purchase as the buyer was a PLC and the information was market-sensitive. And then one day we had to tell them what had happened. We got them all into a pub in north London and told them they had been sold. People were in tears. A week after the sale, I'd have happily torn up my seven-figure cheque and gone back to how things were.

I'm glad I didn't, though. The money was nice – and the sale worked. The new buyer (Hoskyns, now part of Capgemini) proved a good place for our people. Many stayed on for years in senior positions. Others left, then founded their own businesses. One of the most moving days of my life was a reunion of former Instruction Set employees, years after the sale. Around 50 people turned up.

Other types of sale

Selling to another business, as above, is known as a *trade sale*. There are other exit routes. All the material above, about combining market and personal awareness and about checking the seriousness of suitors, applies to these too.

Initial public offerings

Initial public offerings (IPOs) or 'floats' mean going public on the stock exchange. These sound wonderful – all that money and all that media profile – but behind this glittering surface lurk horrible disadvantages.

One disadvantage is that a sizeable chunk (allow for 10%) of all the value you have carefully built up over the years vanishes one way or other into the pockets of the financial institutions that organise the IPO. Take a walk round your nearest big city financial district and look at the premises these people occupy if you aren't sure whether or not they overcharge for their services.

Another is the people you subsequently have breathing down your neck. Institutional shareholders make even VCs look long-termist. Fund managers get a roasting if their portfolio underperforms for a quarter.

Listing on any exchange tends to involve the company in a web of unfamiliar legal, accounting and reporting rules.

Share prices are volatile, and their movements are often unrelated to your performance. General levels of market enthusiasm rise and fall, as does the fashionability of sectors. Just because the financial community has decided that the area you have spent years mastering is bad business, your company is suddenly at the mercy of all kinds of unprincipled corporate raiders.

And finally, you don't even get to see that wonderful paper wealth you were credited with the day you went public. There are legal requirements about how long you have to hold stock for. Even when these are satisfied, if you sell too much at a time you can set off a market slide. And if the share price has fallen in the meantime . . .

I've heard it argued that PLC status adds gravitas to a company. I prefer the gravitas of healthy profits, happy staff, even happier customers, and a reputation for ethical practice.

Private sale, buy-outs and staying private

A 150-person (or more) company is big enough to talk seriously with VCs about a private sale. Other alternatives include the tier of management below you buying you out, or new managers coming in and doing this.

You need top advisers when considering any of these routes. Not 'good enough' ones, but the very, very best. Their fees will horrify you but consider the cost of getting bad advice at this time.

Some businesses do not exit, and stay private, either in specialist niches or as companies that just keep growing. If you can manage this, it is lovely. Not because it makes you mega-rich, but because private companies can concentrate on what really matters – working with great people to create amazing products that continue to delight their customers – without having to dance to the tune of fund managers, big corporate owners, VCs or stock exchange bureaucrats.

Successful private companies include Bechtel, Cargill, Levi Strauss and Mars. Much of Germany's world-beating manufacturing sector is made up of them. If you have a Bosch or a Miele washing machine, it was made by a private company. Virgin Group went public, then hated it so much that it bought itself back into private ownership again.

Whatever route you follow, it is imperative that the top team has thought about the matter and has agreed on its preferred exit route. You cannot afford to have disunity on this issue. The best way to avoid disunity is to discuss the issue early on in the oak stage, and to keep revisiting it, not to refuel greed but to ensure everyone knows where they are going. 'So we get big, what do we do then?'

Winning for real

Enterprise is a bit like mountaineering. Half the skill is getting to the top; the other half is getting back down again in one piece. Be Hilary or Tenzing, not Mallory or Irvine.

You've been well off before you sold (or before you stayed private and started building a large private company), with a good salary and/or dividend pay-outs. Now you have serious money. Sadly, this doesn't always bring the happiness you expect.

You can lose friends. Some people you thought were friends will become jealous. They'll ask for money, and either not be particularly grateful if you give it to them or be nasty if you don't. Hint: don't give any. The best way to avoid embarrassment is to have a fabulous celebration with your friends, at which you all have a great time (paid for by you), but at which you also say you have decided not to do anything with the money for a while, to get used to how things are. Add that you're sure this won't damage the friendship.

Extended family can also turn into self-righteous vultures at this time.

Beyond family, there are all kinds of nasties out there waiting to pounce. If you publicly get rich, you will start hearing endless sob stories. A few of them might even be true. There are also many tales of successful entrepreneurs being entrapped by gold-diggers, scammers or blackmailers.

There are nasties inside too. We all have dark sides to our character. The problem is that up to a point these can be helpful in building a business. They can give us drive, they can give us rage against fate when things go wrong. They can give us harsh insight into rivals who lack Beermat scruples about how they do business. But in the long run, they are destructive to ourselves and to others around us. Some entrepreneurs are still trying to convince a sceptical 'inner parent' who still complains that they're not good enough, even though the business is now worth £10 million. Such a psychological tormentor won't be happy when it's £100 million, either. Others want to be famous as well as rich, but fame is even harder to handle than wealth.

Having harnessed these darker forces to propel you to wealth, it's now time to turn and face them. You can do so with gratitude, which most therapists say is a powerful tool in disabling inner nasties. And then you can let them go. Time for coaching and personal development work.

The alternative can be deeply unpleasant. I worked (briefly) with one successful entrepreneur who went down a spiral of degeneration ending in death. The spiral had two strands to it, ironically like the two spiralling strands that create life. One was simple consumption fever, beginning with the obligatory Ferrari. The other was abuse of personal power. Like many entrepreneurs, this person was manipulative, but he began to get an active kick out of pushing people around. Just how far can you make people jump for money? This soon extended to the sexual area. Allegations of rape were made, then suddenly dropped. At the same time, his consumption turned to drugs. Eventually the police got wind of this and searched his house. Crack cocaine was found, allegedly enough for them to charge him for dealing. He ended up taking two other people for a spin in his latest, mega-expensive car and smashing it into a tree. Nobody survived.

That's an extreme story, but it's true (and well documented in various media just in case anyone thinks I'm overdramatising).

Winning for real is very different. It is about gaining wealth and power, and about not letting them take away your common sense and common kindness. This may be the final gift your mentor can give you – as a role model of how to become rich and successful with dignity and grace.

Winning is about knowing that the people who helped you get rich have benefited too – hence the importance of the stock options scheme. Stock options are less obviously of value if you stay private. You can still give people shares in the company, but a generous bonus scheme is probably more appropriate here.

Winning is about knowing you have created something new and different, which has benefited many people including your customers, but also anyone whose life has been improved by your product – maybe only in small ways, but over time the amount of good adds up. There are enough destructive forces in the world out there. Maybe, if the second law of thermodynamics is true, they will win in the end. You have done your unique bit to combat them, to create and build.

You have fulfilled your own potential too. If you have defied entropy publicly, you have also done so in yourself. Society is full of forces pushing us into various boxes, seeking to define, control and predestine. You have created an identity for yourself that has overcome these forces.

Winning is also about a good night's sleep, about knowing that you haven't done all this by hurting innocent people on the way up. All through this book I have stressed the value of fair, open, ethical dealings with people – with employees, with competition, with society. I believe there is real commercial pay-off to this way of doing business, but it also has the benefit of keeping your conscience intact.

Finally, I believe that winning means putting something back after you have cashed in. Spread some good karma.

I have done this through mentoring. I'll give an hour of my time to anyone who asks politely and who is prepared to fit into my schedule.

I also hope I've put something back through the book – and that this edition will carry on the tradition.

Even my post-sale extravagance gave something back. I created a seventies revival band and made sure it was top class. I had people come up to me after gigs and say they'd just had the best evening ever. The band was set up to entertain, not to make money. Profits were ploughed back into horn sections and light shows, which created work for musicians and technicians who could then go off and create great art if they felt like it, and also provided extra entertainment for audiences. And an extra ego-boost for me, of course. But that's the point. The situation was win–win, like all good business practice.

Creating win–win outcomes is what it has been about all along – from that very first sale. There used to be a kind of castor oil morality in Britain: if something hurt, it was good for you. In the business world, it led people to put up with appalling customer relations and appalling industrial relations. Neither of these is acceptable any more. We have to put effort into creating and developing win–win situations, with customers and staff, not just looking after number one and enjoying a good whinge when someone gets one over on us.

The Beermat entrepreneur is a winner!

- Wealth!
- . . . taken with dignity and grace
- . . . and shared out fairly among the people who most helped you create that wealth
- Many people's lives improved
- Your own potential fulfilled
- A clear conscience: You fought 'hard but fair'
- Putting something back once you have succeeded: Helping others win too

---

I wish you every success in your business career. Follow the patterns I've outlined in this book. Stay positive. Love the journey, with all its ups and downs – and, I hope, the fruits of success.

Perhaps my favourite entrepreneur story is of a friend with whom I spent many hours sitting in a pub (where else?) talking about various business plans. He eventually founded a software company and made a lot of money out of it. We lost contact, but a while ago I got in touch with him and he suggested meeting at that same old pub. We did, and half way through a delicious meal there I commented on how much nicer the place had become since the old days.

'It's improved a lot since I bought it,' he explained.

Appendix

The Magic Email

This is a formula for the email I suggest sending out to researched prospects at level two in the Beermat sales funnel (see Chapter 2). There are five key aspects to it which translate into four *brief* paragraphs plus the all-important subject heading.

1 *'I notice . . . '* Use any information you have about the prospect here. 'I noticed that ABC has recently moved to new offices in Preston.' Or personal information. 'Congratulations on your appointment as COO of MicroCorp.'

2 *Pain and premise.* The basic pain you solve and how you do it.

3 Your *proof.* A customer recommendation.

4 Finally, of course, you ask for a *meeting.* Always offer to visit the customer. It takes less of their time but also gives you an invaluable chance to take a peek at their organisation: is it buzzing or half-asleep? Suggest a time.

5 The *subject heading.* A well-written email will get you a long way, but it is no use if nobody opens it. You must have a compelling heading. If you have a personal endorsement from a respected industry player, that's the ideal one: 'Recommendation from Joanna Evans'. The recipient will spot the name and open the mail. (Of course, you *must* check with your 'magic email endorser' that they are happy to be used in this way. It is a step beyond a simple endorsement, and they may not agree.)

If this option is unavailable, then revert to your information. 'Heard the news about Midicorp' or 'Congratulations on your appointment.' The generic 'Save money with this new app' is a no-no, of course. You can do better than that. And you'll avoid those things that spam filters pick up, like sentences beginning with Free, CAPITALS and loads of exclamation marks at the end!!!

> Subject: Referral from Joanna Evans
> cc.   Joanna Evans
>
> Dear Mr Jones
>
> I noticed from your website that Amalgamated Data has just opened a branch in Cardiff. Congratulations!
>
> Joanna suggested I get in touch as we do the web design for Cymru Technology. They wanted a site that was user-friendly for both English and Welsh speakers. We built one for them and now maintain it. We also help them deal with Welsh-speaking enquiries.
>
> Joanna would be pleased to provide a reference: joanna. evans@*****.com
>
> I'd like to arrange a short meeting. I will be in Cardiff on Tuesday 14th in the morning. Can you spare me 15 minutes?
>
> Regards
> Your Name
> Your Company
> Your Address
> Your Phone
> Any other contact details (etc.)
>
> Disclaimer

Leaving a physical address is all part of making the email 'clean' for the GDPR legislation.

The *disclaimer* is another part of this compliance. I suggest that you ask around for the best form of words to use in it. As I've said, the rules and their accepted practical interpretation are in a state of flux at the moment – so there is no point in my suggesting words that may soon be out of date. The essence of the disclaimer is to assert a) that you are getting in touch because you have a genuine business offer, and b) that if the recipient replies asking to be removed from your records, you will do so at once.

Further reading

Here are our top ten business and entrepreneurship classics. They are not in any order of preference. We go back to these books again and again for inspiration and clarity.

In Search of Excellence by Tom Peters and Robert H Waterman Jr

Crossing the Chasm by Geoffrey Moore

How to Win Friends and Influence People by Dale Carnegie

The Innovator's Dilemma by Clayton Christensen

The E-Myth by Michael Gerber

Weird Ideas that Work by Robert Sutton

The Tipping Point by Malcolm Gladwell

Outliers by Malcolm Gladwell

The 7 Habits of Seven Habits of Highly Effective People by Stephen Covey

Good to Great by Jim Collins

We both enjoy entrepreneur autobiographies too. These give the feel of the start-up life and are good reminders of the qualities needed to drive an idea from something bright on the back of a beermat to a great business. At the same time, remember that entrepreneurs can blow their trumpet rather more loudly than the actual story merits. Other people have usually played more of a role in the success than entrepreneur-turned-authors seem to recall. Funny thing, memory . . . However, the thrills and spills are there, and dealing with them is what entrepreneurship (and being a foil, cornerstone or dream-teamer) is most about.

To go deeper into specific aspects of business-building, I suggest our own guides which link in to the Beermat models and ethos. I recommend that everyone in a start-up reads *Sales on a Beermat*, because everyone needs to understand the sales process and to be part of it. Everyone must be an ambassador for the business, even the most reticent technical person (who can represent it to other reticent technical people much better than any salesperson could).

Also read *Finance on a Beermat,* written with two highly experienced SME finance directors. Everyone must understand this material, too.

Arguably, the trio of Beermat Guides should be made up by *Delivery on a Beermat*, but exactly how you deliver varies so much from business to business that this would have been an impossible title to write. There are a number of good books on 'Getting things done'. *Marketing on a Beermat* makes up the trio instead. It is a great introduction to the basics of this discipline. Even the most sales-driven business needs to understand how markets work and how to craft products for them, so this goes on my list, too.

Also from our own stable, Chris' ebook, *Ditch the Drama!*, offers fascinating insights on the psychological material discussed on page 94. *PR on a Beermat* is a fine ebook co-authored with PR expert Louise Third.

Good business books are always appearing. Among the crop of recent ones, Chris and I have enjoyed Robbie Steinhouse's *Mindful Business Leadership*, which is about much more than mindfulness. He has a powerful model of the personal qualities that leaders need. Garry Mumford's *Business by Numbers* deals with SME finance in clear, comprehensible language. *Seven Steps to Improve Your Business Skills* by Neil Mullarkey is an excellent, witty book on developing your personal and interpersonal skills for the workplace – essential for life in the Beermat business.

Our website www.beermat.biz features blogs, podcasts from a range of people in the start-up world, and other Beermat announcements and goodies. Please come and visit us; you'll be most welcome.

The Prince's Trust

The Prince's Trust offers practical and financial support to young people who are looking to start their own business through its Enterprise programme. Included in the support is a mentoring scheme – the best in the country. Applicants who launch their business through the Enterprise programme are assigned a business mentor, who will be available for up to two years.

To be eligible for the programme, you need to be between 18 and 30 as well as currently unemployed or working fewer than 16 hours a week.

The Trust has a comprehensive outreach scheme – but why not just contact it direct? It will take a very proactive approach to you and your business. The easiest way to get in touch is via the website: www.princes-trust.org.uk. If you can't get online, there's a free 0800 number (0800 842 842).

An assistant will speak to you, checking briefly to see if you fit the criteria, and take down basic details. After that, the Trust makes much of the running. It has a local business development manager, who will contact you to arrange a one-to-one meeting and explain what it has to offer and how it works. Essentially, this person will help you develop a business plan, which you will then submit to a panel of volunteers. Don't be put off by the sound of this as the process is usually pretty informal and the panel is there to award support and money. If the panel thinks you and your idea have got what it takes, the Trust can offer:

- loans
- mentoring
- an excellent business support package, including the opportunity to network with other entrepreneurs.

The Prince's Trust has a positive, unpatronising approach. It wants to help. If you think you might be eligible, get in touch with it.

Index

eBay 27, 65
Edison, Thomas Alva 74
80/20 rule 114–15
elevator pitch 29–31
email 46, 167–9
energy sappers 94
Enterprise Allowance Scheme 67
Enterprise Management Incentive
    (EMI) scheme 155
enthusiasm, generating 112
enthusiasts 9
entrepreneurs 90, 91–2
Equality Act of 2010 97
equity meeting 42
ethos 60–3
Etsy 27
Evans, Chris 130
experience 54–5
externally appointed non-exec 153

Facebook 128
fallen angels 120
family 68
farmers 32
Ferrari 121–2
Field of Dreams xviii 44
fifth person *see* critical factor
    cornerstone
finance
    cornerstone 90
    sapling enterprise 118–19
    seedling enterprise 63–5, 84–5
Finance on a Beermat 63, 70,
    119, 124
first customer 31–9
flaky foil 40–1
FMCG (fast-moving consumer goods)
    entrepreneurs 77
foils 8–12
    as enthusiasts 9
    flaky 40–1
    as magnets 9, 10–12
    as makers 9, 10, 11
    as monitors 9, 12
    as personality type 9

former employees, cornering of
    148–52
Fraser, Sir Campbell 55
friend(s) 68
    of mentor 68
Friends Reunited 129
funding
    mighty oak business 153–4
    sapling enterprise 119–22
    seedling enterprise 65–72

globalisation of mighty oak business
    154–5
goal-setting 112
good idea 24–9
    origin of 24–8
    spotting of 28–9
Google 78, 128–9
Google Glass 17
government loans 67
grants 67
Greedometer 107
guardian angels 120

Hanson Trust 11
heads of agreement *see*
    memorandum of understanding
help 130–5
Hitler, Adolf 5
hunters 32

ideas
    getting 55
    into practice, putting 53
    individual, understanding 109–10
influencers 79, 80
initial public offerings (IPOs) 159–60
Insights Ltd 109
Instagram 127
intellectual property (IP), theft of
    63, 73
intimidation 63
intrapreneur 17–18, 85–6
intuition 55–6
investor relations 120